THE WITCH'S SPELLBOOK

THE WITCH'S SPELLBOOK

Enchantments, Incantations, and Rituals from Around the World

Sarah Bartlett

Brimming with creative inspiration, how-to projects, and useful information to enrich your everyday life, Quarto Knows is a favorite destination for those pursuing their interests and passions. Visit our site and dig deeper with our books into your area of interest: Quarto Creates, Quarto Cooks, Quarto Homes, Quarto Lives, Quarto Drives, Quarto Explores, Quarto Gifts, or Quarto Kids.

Inspiring | Educating | Creating | Entertaining

First Published in 2018 by Fair Winds Press, an imprint of The Quarto Group, 100 Cummings Center, Suite 265-D, Beverly, MA 01915, USA.
T (978) 282-9590 F (978) 283-2742 QuartoKnows.com

Fair Winds Press titles are also available at discount for retail, wholesale, promotional, and bulk purchase. For details, contact the Special Sales Manager by email at specialsales@quarto.com or by mail at The Quarto Group, Attn: Special Sales Manager, 401 Second Avenue North, Suite 310, Minneapolis, MN 55401, USA.

21 20 19 18 17   1 2 3 4 5

ISBN: 978-1-59233-823-8

Digital edition published in 2018
eISBN: 978-1- 63159-486-1

The content for this book originally appeared in *Spellcraft for a Magical Year* (Fair Winds, 2015) by Sarah Bartlett.
Library of Congress Cataloging-in-Publication Data can be found under *Spellcraft for a Magical Year*.

Design, illustrations, and page layout: The Lost & Found Dept.

Printed in China

To Jess

CONTENTS

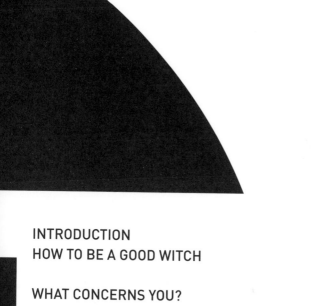

INTRODUCTION

When I was in my early twenties, I worked in London and would spend my lunch hours indulging in one of my favorite pastimes: browsing the dusty shelves of antiquarian bookshops. One warm day in June, my fingers ran across a thin, leather-bound volume with no title; inside, the frontispiece read, *Invocations for the Summer Solstice*. The twenty-four thick parchment pages revealed twelve magic spells to be performed for each hour of the day between dawn and dusk. One spell stood out for me, a spell to get back a lover. (Yes, I'd recently been dumped.) I bought the book.

As the solstice was only four days away, I was tempted to try out the spell the next day. What did a few days' difference matter? Yet scrawled in black ink in the back of the book were the words, *Invoke the right power on the right day, and only then will you have your way*. Impatient as I was to have a go at my chosen spell, I humbly waited for the twenty-first of June and the hour that was set for the spell—3 p.m.

I followed the magic recipe, used the right ingredients, and believed—oh, how I believed that my ex would come running back to me! But an hour or so after I had cast the spell, I felt disillusioned and thought it was just a silly game. Yet two weeks later, my ex phoned to say he'd made a terrible mistake, and could we meet up? Two weeks after that he moved into my flat, and a year later we got married. In fact, that fragile book was not only the trigger for my new life direction as an astrologer practicing the magical arts, but it is the inspiration behind writing this spell book for you.

We all want to lead a magical life—one in which we are able to both shape and take responsibility for our destinies. This book reveals how, by simply casting spells that align with the cycles of nature and the universe, you too can begin to manifest your dreams.

You too can create magic in your life by working with the cycles of nature to help shape your own future. Go out and be united with the stars to help bring you the magical happiness you are seeking.

To every witch reading this book, let the light of the universe shine through you every day.

HOW TO BE A
GOOD WITCH

What you need to know

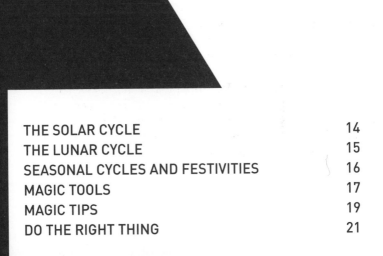

When you think about it, life on earth came into being simply because of our proximity to the sun. As the center of our planetary system, the sun's source of power has a direct influence on both the world around us and the force that permeats all things: magical power. In fact, all of nature is imbued with solar energy, which is why most of the materials used for spell work include crystals, paper, flowers, herbs, and so on.

Still, it was only five hundred years ago that most of humanity believed the Earth was the center of the universe and the sun and planets revolved around it. In the sixteenth century, Polish astrologer Nicolaus Copernicus revived an ancient Greek theory that the Earth rotated daily on its axis and circled the sun. Yet even though astronomers such as Kepler and Galileo knew this theory to be true a century later, the Roman Catholic Church considered it heretical, and it wasn't until the middle of the eighteenth century that it was finally "proved" by science. All these astronomers, or rather astrologers, also believed that there was more to heaven and earth than imagined, a force that permeated and shaped the universe.

This magical force included an established system of correspondences rooted in ancient Egyptian and Greek magical texts, such as the Egyptian Papyrus of Ani (ca. 1250 BCE) and the so-called Greek Magical Papyri—a collection of fragments of parchment from Greco-Roman spell books and magical writings dating from the second century BCE. Correspondences—that is, colors, deities, planets, talismans, plants, herbs, directions, animals, weather patterns, and so on—were all symbolic of one another. Whether sun, rain, earthquake, storm, or volcano, or even an abstract concept such as jealousy, each was identified with a presiding deity or spirit. These gods were associated with the planets, and their corresponding attributes were used in magic potions or worn as talismans to invoke their specific powers. For example, Venus is the closest planet to Earth, and it is associated with love, women, fertility, vanity, and beauty. To the ancients, Venus appeared as both the morning star and the evening star, so it was also thought at times to usher in the dawn, and at others the dusk—as ambivalent as the goddess Venus was thought to be. Going back even further, in Paleolithic times, plants and animals were used to heal, cure, or protect; the use of symbols carved into stone or in cave paintings called on spirits or the otherworld to aid in hunting or fertility, and the natural world and its cycles were respected and honored.

In fact, magic developed from simply a means to get "help" from the powers that be, to an ability to manipulate the energy of the cosmos so that you, the individual, could control your own destiny. By working with talismans, symbols, and correspondences you could also invoke the power of the divine to see into the future, or to make changes in the world. By drawing on the sun's power and magnifying it in your life by using talismans of the solar gods and their associated correspondences—by wearing gold jewelry, lighting candles, and so on—you could keep the power of the sun on your side, ready to help you in your quest.

THE SOLAR CYCLE

Over the course of a year, as the sun appears to move through the sky along an imaginary pathway known as the ecliptic, it crosses the made-up divisions of celestial longitude, which divide the sky into twelve 30-degree slices of a circle (to make up 360 degrees). In astrology, these twelve sectors were named after the constellations—Aries, Taurus, Gemini, Cancer, Leo, Virgo, Libra, Scorpio, Sagittarius, Capricorn, Aquarius, and Pisces—and are known collectively as the zodiac, a system originally developed by Babylonian astronomers in the seventh century BCE. Strangely, as the sun "moves" through these areas, a different energy can be felt, as if the sun, planets, and their alignment to Earth create a different atmosphere throughout the year. This is one of the reasons why people born under a certain zodiac sign are said to be influenced by the qualities of that sign. For example, the sign of Aries, ruled by the planet Mars, is associated with fire, impulse, self-concern, and aggressive energy, as well as the first growth of spring, virility, and an outgoing nature. When the sun moves through the next sign, Taurus, it is ruled by Venus, and so the solar energy is associated with femininity, sexual pleasure, and indulgence.

The sun gives life. It permeates us all at some level, whether physical or spiritual. By working with this solar energy, and by harnessing the power of specific deities and their correspondences who resonate to the solar period, you can work to help manifest your desires.

THE LUNAR CYCLE

Another important cycle in the calendar year is that of the moon, which is also shrouded in magical association. Thought to be the territory of magic and sorcery goddesses such as Hecate and Selene, it has its own unique energy, especially when full—when "lunatics" appeared to be under the moon's spell, its strange nocturnal light was associated with werewolves, dark powers, and evil. But the moon also symbolizes regrowth and spiritual truth, new beginnings, romance, art, and the beauty of silver. Many religions, such as Hinduism, still base their year on the varying lunar phases.

The moon has four phases lasting approximately 29.5 days total. These phases are the new moon, best for beginning new projects; the waxing moon, between the new moon and full moon, best for spells concerning growth and creativity; the full moon, the perfect night for fulfilling spell work, when witches celebrate the "esbat" in honor of the moon goddess; and the waning moon, between full moon and dark new moon, best for slowing down, finishing off projects, and casting spells for banishing or releasing energy.

SEASONAL CYCLES AND FESTIVITIES

No matter where you live, the seasons change—in some places more dramatically than others. This is dependent on the tilt of the Earth and its relationship to the sun. In ancient times, weather was held responsible for life or death, fertility and growth, the harvest and the dormant season. In many traditions, the deities associated with the weather were invoked to increase or diminish their seasonal power. Similarly, you can use magic to tap into the power of the seasons and their gods to invoke the right energy for improving your own life and journey. You can work with these energies at any time of year, but by using them at the allotted period, you increase your chances of success tenfold.

It was often because of the seasonal, planetary, or universal energy changes that worldwide cultures held traditional festivities marking these changes, such as the time for harvest, the fertility rites of springtime, the Chinese New Year, the Roman festival of Cybele, and so on. Just as you can hone your spell casting with the seasons by harnessing the power of these important moments and dates, and using ingredients and rituals associated with these times, you will be in harmony with the goals or destiny you envisage for yourself.

MAGIC TOOLS

A few magic tools are also an essential part of a witch's stock. However, you don't have to buy any of these; they can all be found at home, or used in a symbolic way. A wand can be your favorite pen; an athame, a kitchen knife; a chalice, a pretty cup; or a cauldron, your aluminum pan.

ALTAR

It isn't always possible to have a permanent altar in your home. You can perform most of the spells in this book on a table, but if you can, create a sacred space or corner of a room—even if it's just a window ledge. You'll then be ready to practice creative rituals and spells in your special place.

Altars usually consist of a flat surface covered with cloth. A pair of candlesticks, a picture of your favorite deity, and a selection of crystals or magic charms that mean something personally to you can be placed on the altar at the back, with enough room at the front for casting spells.

WAND

The wand is symbolic of the element Air and is used to point to the spirits of the four directions or to cast a protective circle around you. It can be made from a stick, twig, or even a roll of paper. Be creative and carve your stick with symbols, such as glyphs or runes, or words sacred to you.

ATHAME

An athame is a ceremonial dagger, with a double-edged blade and usually a black handle. It is associated with the element Fire and is often used as a ritualistic tool for pointing at magical ingredients when saying a charm and directing and channeling psychic energy.

CHALICE

A chalice is simply a goblet-shaped container. Associated with the element Water, it is often filled with magical ingredients before a spell is cast. The base is symbolic of the material world, the stem of the connection between man and spirit, and the opening of receiving spiritual energy.

CAULDRON
Cauldrons are simple cooking pots. They are used to combine magical ingredients or as a receptacle for burning away petitions written on paper, once a spell has been set. Representing the element Earth, they symbolize not only the goddess but also the womb.

CANDLES
Most of the spells in this book use candles. They can be any you particularly like, whether votives, tapers, or tea lights, unless a type is specifically mentioned in the ingredient list.

MAGIC TIPS

Many of the spells in this book use simple ingredients such as candles, pen and paper, and a range of symbols, but there are also a few important symbolic components that you should learn to help protect you from negative energy, and to strengthen your contact with the magical world.

DRAWING A PENTAGRAM

Pentagrams are often drawn at the beginning of or during a spell-casting session, as they act as a protective element against any unwanted negativity. The pentagram is associated with all the elements, and the points represent Earth, Air, Fire, Water, and Spirit. Sometimes it also symbolizes love, wisdom, knowledge, law, and power. The Wiccan pentagram is drawn "upright," with the single point on top. This differs from the Satanic, or inverted, pentagram, which has its single point at the bottom.

A magic pentagram is drawn in one line without taking your pen off the paper. This imbues it with magical power, as it is thought that one complete line, like drawing a circle, represents the universe. Once you know how to draw a pentagram, you can also use it as a symbol of power and protection by drawing it in the air before any spell craft. With a pen,

1. *Start at the lower left point of the star.*
2. *Draw a slightly angled line up to start the top point.*
3. *Draw a slightly angled line down to mark the bottom right point.*
4. *Draw diagonally across to make the top left point.*
5. *Cross horizontally straight across to mark the top right point.*
6. *Draw diagonally back down to meet the bottom left point you started from.*

HOW TO CAST THE MAGIC CIRCLE

Magic circles are often used for more complex work because they protect you from a wide variety of unwanted energies, which can get in the way of your spell. Magic circles are best done outside, because you are then drawing directly on the electromagnetic forces of the landscape. You can first practice this at home, but it puts you directly in touch with the magic in nature if you can do it outside. Choose a quiet place, perhaps your garden, in the countryside, in a park, or even on a beach. Take a compass if you aren't very good at working out which direction you are facing!

Facing east, stand upright, extend your right hand, and point your index finger to the ground. As you slowly pivot around, draw an imaginary circle around you on the ground in a clockwise direction until you arrive at the east again. As you draw the imaginary circle, repeat the following:

"I draw this magic circle for protection and to show I am at one with the heavens and the spirits of the four directions."

Next, you have to call in the spirits. With your right hand outstretched again, point your finger to the east and call in the east spirit.

Say,

"I call you, spirit of the East, to help me be touched with inspiration and innovative ideas."

Repeat this charm in each of the other three directions, doing so in a clockwise direction: from the east, call in the spirit of the south, then the west, and finally the north.

Now that you have called in the spirits, stand quietly for a moment in the center of your magic circle and quietly prepare yourself for the next stage of whatever spell you are working with.

DO THE RIGHT THING

Spell work first begins with your own moral responsibility when performing magic. When you perform any magic spell or enchantment, you must be honest with yourself and accept that you are doing it not only for the good of yourself, but also for everyone else. "What goes around comes around," according to the law of witchcraft, and ill intentions sent out may be visited upon you—usually threefold. So remember, never cast spells in a moment's impulse, in anger, or to hurt or upset others. Each time you cast a spell, think about your motives: Are they with goodwill, with no intentions of hurting anyone else?

Every time you work with the magical world, accept that there are unseen powers that may be difficult to contact. This is why performing spells at certain times of year creates the right interface between you, the spell, and the magical powers of the heavens. As witches, we must respect the workings of the universe and its magic, and it may be that at times we simply didn't quite get it right. (Perhaps we just didn't believe in the magic enough for it to work.) What you must never do is worry or dwell on spells that don't work. Rather, move on, try again, and most of all find deep within yourself a real sense of belief. The next time, you will succeed.

When casting spells, you must truly believe in the magic of the universe. You must truly believe that what you are doing is going to work and that you're going to make something beneficial happen. Once you have accepted this, you will be quickly on your way to creating spells that will help you to form your own destiny, just as you want it to be.

WHAT
CONCERNS
YOU?

YOUR SELF

Who would you like to be?

FIND YOUR LIFE DIRECTION

AN ENCHANTMENT CALLING ON BONA DEA
When to Perform This Spell: The Feast of Bona Dea (December 4)

Bona Dea was a Roman earth goddess associated with fertility and abundance. As mother earth, she was invoked or worshipped during important rites of passage, such as birth, entering adulthood, and death. Because she represents change and growth, invoke her powers to alter your life direction in the way you want.

What You Will Need

6 small pieces of mystic topaz
2 green candles
1 white candle
1 red candle
1 yellow candle

First, place one piece of topaz in a drawer in the room where you spend most of your time. This will encourage lucrative energy for business success.

Lay out the remaining five pieces of topaz in the shape of the points of a pentagram (page 19) anywhere in your home where they won't be disturbed.

For five evenings in a row, light a candle (see below for candle colors) and place it next to a point on the pentagram. Start with the top point on the first night and move in a clockwise direction each night after. Let the candle burn for ten minutes while you gaze at the pentagram and repeat these words,

"Thank you, Bona Dea, for your power.
With this help, my life will flower."

After ten minutes, blow out the candle and leave it in its place.

Night one: Green candle
Night two: White candle
Night three: Red candle
Night four: Yellow candle
Night five: The second green candle. This time say,

"Thank you, Bona Dea, for what will come.
Abundance draws powers from the Sun
And with this topaz, Five is One
For what is turned, can't be undone."

Place the five stones in a pouch, keep it in a safe place, and then remove the candles.

VITALIZE PERSONAL POWER

A SPELL CALLING ON YOUR ANCESTORS
When to Perform This Spell: Ghost Festival (August 16)

During the Ghost Festival, the Chinese celebrate the dead, including ancestors believed to return to the world as ghosts. Ritualistic food offerings and elaborate gifts are prepared for the visiting spirits, who are left an empty seat at the table, and incense is burned. This spell uses ingredients that invoke the help of your own friendly ancestors.

What You Will Need
A bell
Sandalwood incense
Salt
A small bowl of olive oil
A small glass of wine
A small spoon

Place all your ingredients on the table or altar, then cast an imaginary magic circle around you as explained on page 19. As you cast the circle, say,

"I invite all spirits and energies to remain who are happy and a good influence to me. I banish all those energies and spirits who are negative and ask you to depart now."

Now ring the bell five times to welcome the good spirits of your ancestors. As you do, say,

"All spirits and ancestors that love me truly, be welcomed here, so mote it be."

Light the incense and sprinkle salt into the bowl of oil while you say,

"By the elements and ancestral spirits, I purify and vitalize myself."

Pour the wine into the bowl, gently stir your alchemical mixture with the spoon as you close your eyes, and say,

*"By alchemy, by spirits true
My ancestors now come to me
To always help and give resolve
To empower my world and bring me love."*

Finally, thank your ancestors:

"Thank you, all spirits and ancestors, the spell is done, now return with love, and all be gone."

Leave the magic potion for one night and then pour it away in the morning, and your whole being will be empowered with fresh vitality.

BRING TO LIFE YOUR INNER MAGIC

A SPELL CALLING ON RHIANNON
When to Perform This Spell: Day of Rhiannon (September 18)

Rhiannon was a lady of Welsh legends who slowly rode a white stallion, luring a love-struck prince who could never catch up with her. Invoked for love spells in medieval times, this enchantment is meant to bring to life your own inner magic, often neglected at the expense of doing magical work "outside" of ourselves.

What You Will Need
You

Sit in a quiet place, preferably cross-legged with your back straight. Close your eyes and calm your mind by breathing slowly, counting down each in-breath from twenty to one.

Once relaxed, put your hands together so the ends of the fingers of each hand touch each other and hold about 5 inches (12.5 cm) away from your chest. Now gradually move your hands, in the same position, to a point just below your belly button. Your hands should sense a change in energy.

This point just below your belly button, called the hara, is often referred to as the body's center of power, the place where you are connected to the spiritual or supernatural realms.

Now stand up, facing east. Spread your arms wide and, with the palms of your hands upward, say,

"All that is One,
All that is the universe within and without,
Eternal and infinite,
Let me be in touch with the true life force that is mine
That I may love myself and trust in my instincts
And to know that as a child of the universe,
Like Rhiannon, I have the power of magic too."

In a gradual sweeping motion, move your hands from the top of your head to your toes. Raise your arms again to the sky and visualize the universal energy being drawn in and down to your magical power center. Don't rush; just enjoy the feeling of welcoming the universal magic to link to your inner being. Repeat the chant three times.

Finally, place your hands with fingers touching each other just hovering over your hara and feel the sizzling energy of your connection to the universe.

ENHANCE CHARISMA

A GENERAL SPELL CALLING ON SELENE
When to Perform This Spell: The Eve of the Full Moon

There are times when we just want to feel good about ourselves, to feel we have the charisma of a star. The word *charisma* originates from an ancient Greek word meaning "divine gift." With a little help from the moon goddess, Selene, you too will be filled with charisma and attraction.

On your altar or a table, create a triangle or pyramid with the three candles (white on top, black on the left, pink on the right). Light the candles. While they burn, sprinkle the rose petals into the bowl of spring water and set it on your altar. Wait for five minutes, then one by one, remove the rose petals and place them on the table. As you do so, repeat the following:

What You Will Need

1 white candle
1 black candle
1 pink candle
5 rose petals
A bowl of spring water
Favorite perfume

"With each petal my beauty grows
Within, without, and all about
Hair, skin, face, and inner wealth
As divine as the goddess, wild but svelte."

Now return the rose petals to the bowl, with a little perfume added. Anoint the potion with a rose petal behind your knees, inner elbows, wrists, neck, and temples. As you do so, say,

"By the power of cosmos, moon, and sun
By the power of three be done
By the power of three, times two and three
As I will, so mote it be."

Only on the eve of the full moon, pour the remaining mixture away. As you do so, repeat the spell,

"Thrice I have charisma fine.
Thrice this beauty will be mine.
Thrice I shine, and thrice I win.
Both those to me whose love they'll bring."

For the next two months, you will find your charisma brings you the attention or attraction factor you are seeking.

BE SEDUCTIVE

AN ENCHANTMENT CALLING ON SISINA
When to Perform This Spell: Flores de Mayo (May 31)

Flores de Mayo is a Catholic flower festival held in the Philippines to honor Sisina, the ancient Filipino goddess of beauty and love whose symbols include white doves' eggs. This charm works to bring Sisina's magic to life in your home and to give you seductive powers and charisma.

First, blow out the inside of the egg. Using the thick needle, carefully pierce a hole in both ends of the egg, making one hole larger than the other. Push the needle into the egg yolk gently and swirl it around carefully to break up the yolk. Hold the end of the drinking straw to the smaller hole and blow through the larger hole to push out the egg white and yolk. Make sure the bottom hole faces the floor so gravity can help. Leave the egg to dry out overnight.

What You Will Need
1 large, white egg
A thick needle
A drinking straw
Red paint or a red pen
White embroidery thread or thin wool thread

When your egg is empty and thoroughly dried out, paint or draw five pentagrams (see page 19) on the shell.

When the paint has dried, thread the thin white thread through the two holes and secure it with a large knot at one end.

Clear your mind, relax, focus on your desire for charisma, and say,

"Little charm made of shell
As you rest here all be well.
May charisma flow to me
May Sisina's power encompass me
May all I do and think and be
Be blessed with grace and love
So mote it be."

Now hang or attach the egg in front of a mirror, where it will reflect and magnify your charisma back to you. This way you can invoke Sisina's magical powers whenever you look at yourself in the mirror.

EMPOWER YOURSELF

AN EQUINOX SELF-EMPOWERMENT CHARM
When to Perform This Spell: Autumn Equinox (September 21)

As day and night are equal on the autumn equinox, this is a time to focus on your own inner balance. This ancient spell from a medieval grimoire will empower you with inspirational energy, making you ready to move forward into the next season of the year, invigorated and ready for action.

What You Will Need

7 pieces of beryl
1 red candle
7 pieces of obsidian
A cardboard box with a lid (optional)

Lay the seven pieces of beryl, which bestow sharp thinking and clarity, on your altar or table in the pattern of the magic symbol Rubeus (see right). This is a potent symbol of power, assigned by Cornelius Agrippa to the zodiac sign of Scorpio, the sign of personal power.

In the gap between the top two crystals of the symbol layout, place the red candle, representing passion. It will invoke zestful fire energy.

Light the candle and repeat this affirmation seven times:

"I will rediscover my own power and will believe in my own light."

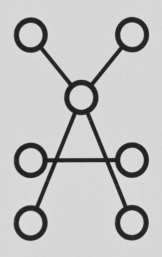

Wait for the candle to burn at least halfway down before you put it out and leave the room. Leave the symbol and candle in place until the equinox day and night are over. The following day, place seven pieces of obsidian (for self-confidence) in the Rubeus symbol pattern in the cardboard box or bury it in the garden with the top of the symbol pointing north to activate the power of the element Water. Leave for two full moon cycles to maximize personal power, then remove the stones and keep them in a safe place.

RADIATE SELF-ESTEEM

AN ENCHANTMENT FOR REVIVAL AND EMPOWERMENT
When to Perform This Spell: Diwali (November 1–20)

Diwali, the start of the Hindu new year, is celebrated by offering basil to the goddess Dharani to ensure future happiness. Planetary positions are also important, so perform this spell during the dates above to ensure the lunar calendar's specific energy. This spell is for empowerment, shaking off the past, bringing life to stagnant projects, and reviving things you once believed ruined.

What You Will Need
Rosewater, jasmine, and sandalwood essential oils or perfumes
7 basil leaves

Start by taking a ritual bath or shower with the perfumed oils to purge your body, mind, and soul of negativity.

After, take the seven basil leaves and place them on a table in a circle.

Next, call upon the energy of the planets. Each time you do so, take one of the basil leaves to represent the planet and place it outside of the circumference of the circle.

"I call on Mercury, the planet of wisdom, to help me transform my beliefs.
I call on Venus, the planet of love, to help me with acceptance.
I call on Mars, the planet of initiative, to give me the drive to act.
I call on Jupiter, the planet of opportunity, to give me the courage to transform.
I call on Saturn, the planet of preservation, to keep me on my path.
I call on the moon, the planet of dreams, to make my wishes come true.
I call on the sun, the planet of success, to fulfill my goals."

You will now have a bigger circle of leaves. Take one leaf, any one that you like the look of, and eat it. This will invoke Dharani's energy and align you with the planetary energy of the day.

Finally, give thanks to Dharani, and very soon you will be able to transform your world.

BE MORE SELF-SUFFICIENT

AN ENCHANTMENT CALLING ON DURGA
When to Perform This Spell: Feast of Durga (September 5–16)

The legend of Durga, the Hindu mother goddess, tells of her great battle with the demon Mahishasura, who shape-shifted into buffalo, lion, elephant, and buffalo again before being beheaded by Durga's trident. Her attributes are silver and gold, and in some regions of India, Durga is invoked to encourage wealth and self-sufficiency into the family.

What You Will Need

4 green candles
1 white candle
10 bay leaves
2 green fluorite stones
10 coins
A silver or metal dish or bowl
A photo of yourself

On your table or altar, make a magic circle with the candles by placing the four green candles at each cardinal point (north, south, east, west) and the white candle in the center. Put the bay leaves, fluorite stones, and coins into the bowl and place this to the right of the circle.

Place your photo in front of the candles.

Light the white candle and then the four green candles. Now take up your photo and gaze at your image while you concentrate for a minute on what wealth and security mean to you.

Still looking at your image, say this charm five times to invoke the magic number of the circle and Durga's powers:

"Security is coming soon to me,
Wealth is flowing unto me,
The power of self-reliance for all to see,
Durga, great goddess, send to me,
Let it come, so mote it be."

Now sit for a few minutes and visualize opportunities coming to you to increase your income, or how you could have all you need to be happy. The longer you can hold this happy image in your mind, the better. Once you feel in an empowered state of mind, replace the photo, blow out the candles, and place the silver bowl of magic ingredients before you.

Run your fingers through the bay leaves and fluorite stones in the bowl to stir up their magical powers to bring you wealth.

Next, take the coins from the bowl and scatter them randomly on the floor in a corner or part of your room where they won't be disturbed for three lunar cycles. As you scatter them, say,

"Scatter money on the floor
Happiness comes back through the door.
Thank you, Durga, for your charm
From now on to us comes no harm."

For the next few months, repeat this little charm in your head every time you need to make a financial or lifestyle decision, and Durga will continue to bless you with happy opportunities and a true sense of self-sufficiency.

ENCOURAGE HEALTH

A HEALTHY LIFE SPELL
When to Perform This Spell: Any time

We all want to be healthier. This spell won't cure you from any disease or ailment, nor will it stop you from catching a common cold, but its magical properties will boost your holistic health.

Place the three basil leaves and angelica powder in the bowl. Prick your finger with the needle and let a drop of blood fall onto the powder.

What You Will Need

3 basil leaves

1 teaspoon angelica root powder

A small glass dish or bowl

A sterilized needle

1 white candle

Do not mix the magic potion or touch it, but simply say the following:

"As without, so within
As above, so below
As with soul, so with skin
As with spirit, so with blood."

Now light the white candle and drip a few drops of wax onto your mixture by tipping the candle at an angle. Say,

"As with energy, so with flow
As with blood, so with sweat
As with body, so with spirit
So with my soul's wealth now enriched
So my body's health will flourish."

At some point in the next three days, empty the contents of your magic potion into a stream, river, or the sea.

Within one lunar cycle, you should feel the energy you need for a healthier lifestyle. If not, repeat the spell, but most of all believe, believe, and believe it as you perform the charm.

RESTORE HOLISTIC HEALTH

A SPELL USING AN OAK TREE
When to Perform This Spell: Oak Apple Day (May 29)

The oak tree is a symbol of longevity, strength, and stability. An ancient Welsh belief holds that good health is maintained by rubbing your hands on a piece of oak, while others believe that dew found under oak trees is a magical beauty aid. This spell is based on one of the charms in Arthur Gauntlet's grimoire *A Cunning Man's Book of Charms*.

What You Will Need
A handful of lavender flowers
Lavender oil
An image of an oak tree
One acorn

Fill your bathtub with warm water, the lavender flowers, and a few drops of the lavender oil. Place the image of the oak tree where you will be able to see it from your bathtub.

Hold the acorn in your right hand and say:

"Cleanse my spirit, cleanse my soul
Enrich my life and make me whole."

Place the acorn beside the picture of the oak tree, then climb into the bath and relax, breathing in the scent of the lavender. Gaze at the imagery of your oak tree and keep repeating to yourself how strong, secure, and beautiful the tree is. Then think of your life in that way too: safe, secure, and whole.

Leave the oak tree image and the acorn overnight. The following morning, place them on your altar or table and then take the acorn between your hands and say,

"This oak tree strong, this oak tree proud
Will always hold us in the ground.
Blessed oak, sacred oak
So mote it be."

Keep the acorn in a special box, and you will feel whole and strong as an oak tree. If you ever feel weak or unwell, hold the acorn and repeat the last part of the spell to restore your strength.

BE YOUTHFUL

AN ENCHANTMENT FOR MIND AND BODY
When to Perform This Spell: As the Sun Moves into Gemini (May 21)

The Gemini twins symbolize youthfulness, and the sun's move into Gemini is the perfect time to attend to your fitness—to look, think, and feel good. In ancient Greece, ribbons were knotted to invoke one's own personal energy as part of the spell, rather than just calling on the gods. This spell works on this principle, so that each knot you make is a symbol of your youthful new self.

What You Will Need

3 lengths (about 3 feet [90 cm] long) of yellow ribbon (Gemini's color)

1 piece of lavender or a lavender pillow

Braid the three strands of ribbon together with five crossings and knot the end. If you don't know how to make a three-strand braid, then just make five knots along the lengths of ribbon.

Between your hands, take hold of the first crossing or knot and say,

*"Gemini's magic is a potent way
For the youthfulness I wish today."*

Move your hands on to the next crossing or knot and say,

*"Oh, Gemini, ribbons help my body be fit
Braided this way, let the spell be writ."*

Move your hands to the third crossing or knot and say,

*"Let the spell grow and my health improve
Thrice times this number my body be true."*

On the fourth crossing say,

*"By the grace of the planets this spell be worked
And my fitness and youthfulness ever alert."*

On the final knot or crossing say,

*"Bound again the spell begins
When in two weeks untied, the spell will be mine."*

Keep the braided or knotted ribbons in a drawer with your clothes along with a piece of lavender or a lavender pillow to enhance the magical qualities of your enchantment. Two weeks later, untie the braid or knots and you will be blessed with a youthful aura and can arrive at the level of fitness that you hope to achieve.

Gemini

BE BEAUTIFUL

A SPELL TO CREATE THE BEST OF YOURSELF
When to Perform This Spell: Amaterasu's Festival (May 5)

Amaterasu, the ancient Shinto sun goddess, once hid in a cave for so long that there was no longer light on earth. Other gods hung a mirror from a tree, and when she peeped out, she saw her reflection. Thinking this was a goddess more beautiful than she, Amaterasu stormed out to confront the rival and thus brought light to the world again. Invoking Amaterasu's magic will give you the ability to create the best of yourself, whether to attract love or simply to know that you are beautiful.

What You Will Need
A hand mirror

Go out for a walk and take the hand mirror with you. Find a café or bench and sit for a while. If the sun isn't shining, imagine it beaming down on you, the solar energy and Amaterasu's magic filling you with light. Take the mirror from your bag and gaze at yourself, even if there are people around you.

Say to yourself, out loud or in your head,

"I am the sun, I am the goddess of the sun, and I am beautiful."

Realize that you are someone special, and then place the mirror back in your bag and walk home.

When you are back in your home, take the mirror and reflect light into every corner of every room. This is the energy you have gathered from the sun, which will empower every inch of your space with magical beauty. You will now be blessed with Amaterasu's qualities and will shine as brightly as she does.

LOSE WEIGHT

A SPELL CALLING ON APHRODITE
When to Perform This Spell: During a New Moon

Magic won't provide a simple way to lose weight, but it can harness Aphrodite's power to help you change your diet, resolve personal issues, feel motivated to exercise, and more. As the goddess of love, beauty, and vanity, Aphrodite's body was her shrine. By invoking her powers, your body too will be blessed with the perfect figure that's right for you.

What You Will Need

A hand mirror

Lavender oil

1 white candle

2 pieces of white quartz crystal

A piece of paper and a pen

Place the mirror where you can see your reflection as you sit before the table. Place a little lavender oil on your fingers and gently rub the oil down the sides of the white candle. Next, light the candle, take a piece of white quartz crystal in each hand, and say,

"Aphrodite, Lady of confidence
Love, esteem, and vanity,
Please help me to see my inner beauty
Reflected before me
And to restore my integrity
Of self-love, body, and soul."

Place the quartz crystals in front of the mirror, one to represent your body, the other to represent your desire to lose weight. While the candle burns, write down the things in your life that make you crave food.

Last, write down these empowering enchantments:

"Food has no power over me."

"My self-respect and self-love are mine."

"I deserve to shine my beauty on the world."

Gaze at yourself in the mirror and say the charms nine times. Thank Aphrodite for her help, then relax for nine minutes while the candle burns, and blow it out. Place the two pieces of quartz crystal under your pillow to empower you to succeed in your goal. Every night before bed—until you reach your desired weight—repeat the three empowerment enchantments while gazing at yourself in a mirror.

CHANGE
What would you like to do?

TAKE CHARGE OF YOUR LIFE

AN ANGEL SPELL CALLING ON SAINT MICHAEL
When to Perform This Spell: The Feast of Saint Michael (September 26)

Michael, the warrior saint, defeated all evil. Call on him to help you overcome the demons of self-doubt, stress, emotional tension, and negative thoughts and replace them with dedication to yourself. The magic ingredients of spiced wine were often used in seventeenth-century grimoires to call on the angels, who, according to legend, took a sip of the potion before returning to their heavenly domain!

What You Will Need

A piece of paper
A pen
2 glasses of red wine
A cauldron or cooking pot
1 teaspoon cardamom
1 teaspoon cinnamon
5 cloves
A spoon

On a piece of paper, draw a circle and then a square around the outside of the circle. In each corner of the square, write the name of Michael and in the center of the circle write your name.

Pour the red wine into your cauldron or cooking pot and heat gently until simmering, then add the spices and the paper. Let the brew simmer for a few minutes, then turn off the heat and let it cool for one hour. During the hour, write down all the things you want in your life, or those things you long to do or be: to be a better mother or lover; to be empowered with self-belief; to attract good energy; etc.

Most important, exactly seven minutes before the end of the hour (traditionally, angel magic begins at seven minutes to the hour), stir the cauldron and repeat the following:

"Archangel Michael, send out your strength
So that I too can attract goodness into my life.
With this potion stirred once it will be done
This potion stirred twice all evil be gone
This potion stirred thrice my life be fun
This potion stirred last, my empowerment begin."

Bring the mixture to a boil and then turn off the heat.

Spoon a little liquid into a glass, and when cool, take a small sip to honor Michael and mark the beginning of the new, self-empowered you.

DEVELOP A FRESH NEW YOU

A SPELL CALLING ON MAGNA MATER
When to Perform This Spell: The Megalisia (April 4)

Magna Mater, the Roman goddess of world order, was usually depicted alongside tame lions, and her feast was celebrated to acknowledge the power of the gods over mortals. Her benefits included protection from negative influences and flourishing new growth. The Megalisia marked the start of the new agricultural season. Tap into Magna Mater's energy to inspire you and bring you spirited energy.

What You Will Need
A white candle
2 pieces of paper
A black pen
A cauldron or metal cooking pot
1 piece of white quartz crystal

Light the candle and invite the goddess Magna Mater to join you.

"Welcome, Magna Mater. Please join me as I remove all negativity from my life to be empowered with divine and cosmic spirit."

On one piece of paper, draw a pentagram (see page 19).

On the other, write a list of things that you want to banish from your life: for example, fear, addiction, frustration, worry, low self-esteem, jealousy, poverty, depression, etc. Now hold the paper in your hands and say,

"From the lion's paws, comes Magna's charm.
Here on my path she'll be my sweet balm
For her wisdom is great, her protection secure
With her banishing power I will become pure."

In the candle flame, light the paper with the negative words and drop it into the cauldron. As it burns, relax and close your eyes. Imagine and feel your negativity burning away with it. Once most of the paper has burned away, blow out the candle. Now say,

"Thanks be to Magna Mater's light
All is now banished into the night."

Place the white quartz crystal (invokes the power of the universe) in the center of the pentagram and say,

"Thank you, Magna Mater, for leading me away from the dark into the light."

Leave the stone on the pentagram for four weeks (a lunar cycle) to ensure Magna Mater's magic works for you.

Over the next few days, find that all the negative thoughts you once had turn to positive ones, and you can start any new enterprise free of worries.

ATTRACT POSITIVE IDEAS

A SPELL DRAWING ON URANUS
When to Perform This Spell: As the Sun Moves into Aquarius (January 19–20)

As the sun moves into Aquarius, the time dawns to draw inspiration for a prosperous year ahead. This ancient spell will enable you to draw on the power of the planet Uranus, the astrological ruler of Aquarius, while the four spirits who rule the directions will bring you inspiring ideas for a prosperous year while helping you fulfill your goals.

What You Will Need
1 white quartz crystal

First, cast a magic circle around you and call in the four directions that rule the elements Earth (north), Fire (south), Air (east), and Water (west) (see page 19). Sit cross-legged in the middle of the circle with the white quartz crystal in your writing hand. The magical power of the planets will permeate your whole being via the vibrational energy of the crystal. Close your eyes and imagine you are holding out the crystal as an offering, and in turn the planets are sending creative energy into your hands.

Now open your eyes and gaze at the crystal for about a minute, calmly breathing until you have stilled your mind.

Keeping the crystal in your writing hand, use the fingers on your nonwriting hand to touch the crystal as follows and say:

With the thumb:
"By the number 1, the spell's begun."

With the second (index) finger:
"By the number 2, let it be true."

With the third finger:
"By the number 3, so mote it be."

With the fourth finger:
"By the number 4, I won't want for more."

With the fifth finger:
"By the number 5, the spell comes alive."

Repeat this whole number spell five times.

When finished, close your eyes for a minute, breathe slowly and deeply, and close your hand around the crystal, saying,

"Thanks be to the spirits of the East, South, West, and North, and thanks to the planet Uranus for bringing new light to my life."

Place the crystal back on the ground and stand up again. Now, with your right arm outstretched and your finger pointing down, undraw your magic circle by moving slowly around counterclockwise from the east direction until you have completed one turn of the magic circle.

Place the crystal beside your bed or on your desk for five days and nights to maximize the power of this energy. Then put the crystal in a safe place for the rest of the year so the magic can do its work.

Aquarius

MAKE A DECISION

AN ENCHANTMENT CALLING ON THE POWER OF WATER
When to Perform This Spell: As the Sun Moves into Scorpio (October 20)

As the sun moves into Scorpio, Water energy brings flowing thoughts, and like the changing waves and tides of the sea, there is potential in every dream if you go with the flow. This spell draws on the power of the element Water, which in witchcraft is associated with the direction west.

Find a quiet space outside. Stand facing west and draw an imaginary magic circle around you with your wand in a clockwise direction (see page 19).

What You Will Need

A magic wand (a long stick or rod)

A bottle of spring water

A handful of fresh basil, rosemary, and lavender mixed together

A crystal pendulum or a favorite pendant on a chain

Next, you are going to consecrate the west with your water and herbs. Sprinkle some water to the west of you and say,

"To the Waters of the West, I bless and honor your decision-making power."

Now sprinkle some of the mixed herbs in the same place.

Take up your crystal pendulum and concentrate on the decision you want to make. Whatever the question, phrase it so there are only two possible answers, yes or no. Repeat your question over and over in your mind, then stand above the ground where you sprinkled the water and herbs and hold the pendulum steady between your finger and thumb. Close your eyes and keep thinking about this question. The pendulum will start to swing of its own accord: If it swings perpendicularly or horizontally, the answer is no; if it swings in a circle, the answer is yes.

The decision has been made for you by the solar energy of the west. However, if you truly believe that the decision is not right for you, the magic has forced you to trust your deeper instincts and know in your heart what is truly right.

MIRACLE WORKING

A SPELL CALLING ON SAINT BRIGIT
When to Perform This Spell: Saint Brigit's Feast Day (February 1)

Miracle worker Saint Brigit took over the role of Brigit, Celtic goddess of livestock, poetry, sacred wells and springs, and the arrival of early spring. Nuns in Kildare, Ireland, once tended a perpetual flame in her honor. If you want a miracle, usher Brigit's powers into your life using a large old key, symbolizing the one that unlocked Brigit's sanctuary.

What You Will Need

1 red candle

A piece of paper and a pen

1 large old metal key (as large as you can find)

Light the red candle to ignite the energy of Saint Brigit and place it on your altar or table. Next, write down all the things you want to change in your life. Then write down a timeline, or a date in the future you want them to be achieved. Once you have written the list, cross off any that seem totally impossible within your given timeline. Be realistic.

Finally, whittle your list down to one major change by using only one word. It may be just one word, such as *lifestyle* or *work* or *love*, but it will be a *big* word in your mind.

Write down your big word nine times (Brigit's magical number).

Next, charge the key with magic by taking it and slowly drawing it through the flame of the candle from right to left, left to right, nine times total. Keep repeating your "big" word the whole time. Blow out the candle after the ninth pass through the flame. When the key is cool, place it under your pillow for nine nights to fill your life with Brigit's miracle power. The change you seek will be forthcoming within the time frame you wrote down.

HAVE THE COURAGE TO MAKE CHANGES

A SPELL DRAWING ON THE POWER OF LUPA
When to Perform This Spell: The Lupercalia (February 15)

The Roman Lupercalia festival honored Lupa, the she-wolf who suckled the infant orphan founders of Rome, Romulus and Remus. You won't transform into a wolf, but you will draw on the power of the she-wolf so you have the courage to completely change your lifestyle or move on from the past and create a new future.

What You Will Need

1 piece of amber

6 pieces of red/orange carnelian stone

This enchantment uses symbols that harness the Lupercalia's association with creative change and the she-wolf's motif of courageous power. Amber banishes negativity and the carnelian stone, the crystal of courage, fearlessness, and bold action, transforms your life. The hexagram, or six-pointed star, is a potent symbol of both the numinous universe and the manifest one. The upward point is the symbol of the element Fire, while the downward point is the symbol of the element Water. The area in the center of the hexagram is a point of balance and beauty. This is when change can come; this is where you will stand, and where the fearless wolf has the courage to reveal itself.

First, place a piece of amber in a south-facing window of your home to get rid of any negative thoughts and boost your self-confidence.

To activate the spell, place six pieces of carnelian, arranged as the points of a six-pointed star, with enough room for you to stand in the middle. Do this preferably in a garden or outside space or, if necessary, inside your home.

Every day for the next two weeks, step into the middle of the hexagram and repeat the following spell for two minutes with your eyes closed:

"I will change my life, and change will bring me all that I long for."

You will soon be able to see the change that you desire.

ENSURE SUCCESS

A SPELL CALLING ON BRIGIT
When to Perform This Spell: Imbolc Sabbat (February 2)

Imbolc marks the midpoint of winter. It was also when Saint Brigit was said to visit people's homes and they would lay out a special cross with flowers and magical herbs to invoke her power. Follow this old pagan spell to Brigit to ensure changes in your life are successfully completed. You can draw a Brigit cross with four horizontal lines and four interesting vertical lines.

What You Will Need
A Brigit cross or drawing of one
A pouch filled with:
1 piece of amber
(represents Earth)
1 seashell (represents Water)
1 sprig of vervain or mint
(symbolizes Air)
Red rose petals (symbolizes Fire)

Fold the paper with the drawing of the Brigit cross into four, take your pouch, and go for a walk wherever you can be at one with nature. Find a quiet place to sit and relax. Unfold the paper with the cross drawing on the ground and place the pouch on top of it. If you are using a real cross, place it on the ground and put the pouch alongside it. Now invoke the power of Brigit by saying,

"Thank you, Brigit, for bringing successful changes into my life for the rest of the year."

Take up the pouch and one by one remove the elemental symbols—it doesn't matter in which order—placing each on the cross. When the four ingredients are laid out, say,

"By the power of Brigit's delight
I now entertain the right
To be and have and hold and do
All that I want to change anew."

Now say,

"By the power of Brigit, I welcome the big change that is coming my way."

Replace all your elements into the pouch, take up the cross, and return home. Soon your dreams will unfold.

ATTRACT HAPPINESS

A SUMMER SOLSTICE SPELL
When to Perform This Spell: Midsummer's Day (June 20–22)

The summer solstice is one of the most important days in the year for spell work. A time for purification and thanksgiving, we can give thanks for the sunshine and fertility of the past few months and welcome the days where different magic harvests the rewards of the spells sown earlier in the year. This midsummer spell is made up of a ritual to honor the energy, which is best done in the morning of Midsummer's Day, and another spell to perform in the afternoon.

Lay out all the magical ingredients on the altar. Sprinkle some of the herbal oils or essences onto the flowers on your altar, then light the pink candles. Take a few moments to enjoy the fragrances and the flickering flames.

Pick up the athame or wand, hold it firmly in both hands, and visualize all the energy of the sun—perhaps in the form of a warm, golden light—concentrated along its blade.

Hold the blade directly above the bowl of fruit, pointing downward. Visualize the sun's energy passing from the blade into the fruit, which in turn becomes charged with golden energy.

Lay down the athame.

What You Will Need

An altar or table decorated with summer flowers on a white cloth

Lemon balm, lavender, and elderflower essences/oils or perfume

5 pink candles

An athame or wand

A small bowl containing summer fruits you want to eat

Silver rings, diamonds, or white crystal jewelry

Patchouli oil or white musk

A metal goblet or bowl (preferably gold, silver, pewter, or copper colored)

A golden or silver-colored ring

5 white candles

Rose petals

3 cloves

Eat the fruit slowly, giving thanks for the fertility of the sun, while visualizing the fulfillment of all your desires over the coming months. Finally, extinguish the candles.

In the afternoon, wear silver rings, diamonds, or white crystal jewelry and take a bath or shower using patchouli oil or white musk. All these attributes will imbue you with midsummer magic and augment your success for the next six months.

AFTERNOON CHARM

After your ritual bath, take the metal goblet or bowl and the gold or silver ring. These represent Metal magic, the element needed to boost your charisma. Create a magic circle of five white candles and place the bowl/goblet and ring in the center. Next, sprinkle some rose petals into the bowl, followed by three cloves (a magical talisman to represent love, harmony, and peace).

Now light the candles, and as you watch the candles flicker for a few minutes, repeat the spell:

"I am a creature of nature's soul.
These talismans before me my only goal.
Let this midsummer joy my life unfold
And the days to come be as bright as gold."

Blow out the candles and look forward to the enriching months ahead.

MAKE A LIFESTYLE CHANGE

AN ENCHANTMENT CALLING ON ESTSANATLEHI
When to Perform This Spell: The Eve of a Full Moon

Estsanatlehi is the Apache and Navajo name for Changing Woman or Turquoise Woman. Whenever she grows old, she walks east until she sees her younger self, who she then becomes. This spell is about aligning yourself with the power of the four cardinal directions so that you can harness Estsanatlehi's powers of renewal from the east. We often want to make a change in our lives but are loaded down by people, emotions, and worries. With this charm, you can take that step forward and embrace change.

What You Will Need

1 large piece of turquoise

Take the piece of turquoise outside on the eve of the full moon and find a space where you won't be disturbed. First, take the turquoise in one hand and stretch out your arm to the west as if offering it to Estsanatlehi where she lives across the far distant waters. Close your eyes for a moment to relax and calm your mind, then say,

"I embrace change and know it is for the better."

Now turn your body to the north, with hand still outstretched, and repeat the same words, followed by the east and south.

Finally, take the turquoise in both hands and stretch out your arms to the east. Next chant,

"Sky West and crooked her hair falls East
The flames of change lift Earth to North
From the cauldron Silver burns
And Southward flows her gown of Gold
To track the pathways of the Sun
The Moon and Stars will all be One."

Bow to the east and then place the turquoise in your pocket or bag.

Finally, thank the goddess:

"Now I can change my life to whatever I want it to be.
Thank you, Estsanatlehi, for blessing this stone."

Take the stone with you wherever you go, and change will be your friend forever.

KICK AN OLD HABIT

A SPELL FOR STARTING AFRESH
When to Perform This Spell: New Moon in April

April is Venus's month, and invoking the power of Venus will help you to rid yourself of past habits. Venus talismans were worn by Romans not only to deflect the influence of envious or jealous rivals in love, but to banish all past bad influences too, similar to those worn to ward off the "evil eye."

What You Will Need
5 white candles
A small bowl of spring water

For this enchantment, you are symbolically a channel or conduit between time past and future; the present "you" needs to be protected, so first walk in a large clockwise circle with your hand outstretched and pointing at the earth to create a magic circle around you.

As you do so, say,

"I cast this magic circle and am safe between two worlds."

Now within your magic circle, place the five white candles (to represent the five magical elements) in a circle and light them. Then say,

"By the power of earth, fire, water, and air,
Out with the old, in with the new
Blessing, oh Venus, for all that I do
To let go of the past and all that is bad
And empower me with grace and all that is glad."

Sprinkle the water on each of the candles. Finally, blow out the candles, and all past habits you want to leave behind will disappear. In the next few weeks, you can move on from the chains of the past.

STEP OVER A BOUNDARY

A SPELL CALLING ON SATURN
When to Perform This Spell: As the Sun Moves into Capricorn (December 20)

This spell invokes the power of the planet Saturn, ruler of Capricorn, to cross the cusp of your old life and move into a new one. It will enable you to cross any boundary by changing your environment, status, job, or relationships with the energy of today, simply by crossing over a symbolic "high magic boundary" guarded by Saturn.

What You Will Need

A 3-foot (90-cm) length of rope or twine (Or you can twist and knot together pieces of string, rope, or fabric.)

A very large stone or rock

A small cup of corn

A small cup of red wine

Find a quiet place outside. Sit down on the ground and concentrate on the boundary you wish to cross to change your life. It may be a "physical" boundary, such as a career or relationship change, moving abroad, or a financial opportunity. Or it may be an emotional boundary, such as moving away from loss or rejection; giving up an obsession; or desiring to be calmer, more tolerant, more willing, etc. Whatever your personal boundary, accept it now and keep repeating:

"I accept I must cross this boundary. I accept the change that will transform me."

Once you seriously believe this, lay the rope out in a line and place the large stone, representing Saturn, about halfway along. Take the small cup of corn and sprinkle it over the stone. Repeat your mantra of acceptance as you do so. Then say,

"Thanks be, blessed Saturn of night and stars,
To give me wisdom and your prayers.
My goodness let the world to see
My passion, fire, my talents be
To bring me happiness that's now due.
So thrice again I say to you
And thrice again, I say on high
To win gold wings to make this mine
This boundary crossed,
This blockage passed.
I now will move beyond your stone
And win the power of joy alone."

Pour the wine over the stone and repeat your mantra of acceptance.

You are ready to cross the boundary. Take a deep breath and relax. Stand before the rope and take one step over it so that one foot is on either side. Stand like this for a minute, repeating your acceptance mantra as many times as you can. Take your back foot off the ground and place it beside your front foot, crossing the boundary.

The magic will begin to work as you step into the new you, the new world you have created, or simply a new beginning. Now say,

"I have crossed the boundary of transformation and I am now ready to make the change, so mote it be."

This final affirmation is the best magic you can give yourself, but like any of the magic spells here, utter belief in the powers you are invoking is essential for the spell to work!

Capricorn

WISHES

What would you like?

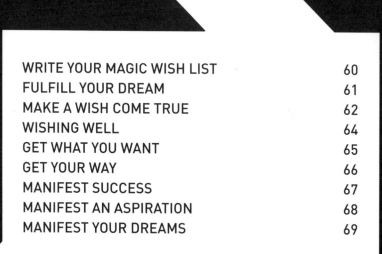

WRITE YOUR MAGIC WISH LIST

A SPELL CALLING ON THOTH
When to Perform This Spell: The Day or Evening of the New Moon

Thoth was the Egyptian god of the moon, wisdom, writing, astrology, botany, mathematics, theology, and all knowledge, human or divine. His knowledge will come through you as you write your magical wish list during the new moon. This is a time of seeding and conception, the moment before a flash of insight or breakthrough, the end or beginning of a cycle.

What You Will Need

1 white candle

A pen and real ink (Thoth's power)

A special piece of paper or parchment

An envelope

Light a white candle to harness the power of the new moon and sit comfortably at a table.

First, write down the following spell:

"With this pen I so inscribe
Desires and wishes as described,
Bring me, Thoth, all that I think
And secure my future with this ink."

Now start to write your wish list, and as you do so, say aloud each wish three times. You can have no more than seven wishes, the magical number of Thoth.

Once you have finished writing, fold the paper, place it in the envelope, and seal it. Now carefully drip a few drops of wax from the candle onto the envelope to bless and seal it with the power of Thoth and to make your wishes come true.

Always be careful what you wish for, because it will manifest before you know it.

FULFILL YOUR DREAM

A SPELL CALLING ON CYBELE
When to Perform This Spell: The Festival of Cybele (March 25)

Cybele was an ancient goddess who, in Greek mythology, rejected Zeus. Eventually Cybele gave birth to Agdistis, a wild hermaphrodite demon the other gods feared so much they cut off his sexual organs. From his blood sprang an almond tree.

Nana, a river nymph, ate the fruit of the tree and fell pregnant. When her son, Attis, became a young man, his grandmother Cybele fell in love with him. However, Attis loved the king's daughter, which made Cybele insanely jealous. Trying to escape Cybele's power, Attis ran through the mountains, stopped by a pine tree, and castrated and then killed himself. From Attis's blood sprang the first violets. Horrified, Cybele called upon Zeus to help resurrect Attis.

What You Will Need

A handful of almonds or 3 drops of pure almond oil

A few violet flowers or 1 tablespoon (15 ml) of violet eau de toilette, perfume, or scent

A silver-colored dish

1 white candle

1 rose thorn

The moral of this story is that we must accept that we can't always have what we want, and that even goddesses are vengeful, irresponsible, and incestuous. However, the positive magic of this enchantment draws on the strength of Cybele's power to bring to life one wish, as she brought to life her beloved Attis.

If you use the oil and perfume method, place the almond oil first in the dish and the perfume afterward. If you use the nuts and flowers method, sprinkle the almonds onto the flowers.

Inscribe your name into the candle with a rose thorn.

Light the candle and place it beside your dish of Cybele's magic ingredients. With your eyes focused upon the flame, concentrate on your wish. When the wish is firmly in your thoughts, whisper the following words three times:

"Great Mountain Mother Cybele, grant my wish. Fulfill my dreams. Smile on me tonight."

Extinguish the candle flame, and within the space of a lunar cycle your wish should be granted.

MAKE A WISH COME TRUE

A SPELL CALLING ON BACCHUS
When to Perform This Spell: Bacchanalia (March 15)

The Bacchanalia consisted of Roman festivals in honor of Bacchus, the Greco-Roman god of wine, freedom, intoxication, and ecstasy. Equivalent to the Greek mystical god Dionysius, each was celebrated at the beginning and end of the grape harvest. This spell uses the magic ingredients associated with both gods to manifest a special wish sooner than you think.

What You Will Need
A piece of paper and a pen or pencil
1 red candle
A cauldron or cooking pot
1 cup (235 ml) red wine and
1 glass of the same red wine or grape juice to drink, if you are averse to wine

Make yourself comfortable and sit before your table or altar of ingredients. Concentrate on what you want to manifest and imagine clearly what it might be like to have it. Write down on your paper what it is you wished for.

Light the candle and focus on the flame, then take up your paper and say,

*"I connect myself to the power of Bacchus
And with this offering give thanks.
So shall this which I have written come to pass.
May it come to me easily, and with harm to none.
I will it. I draw it to me.
I accept it. I receive it. I give thanks for it.
By my will, so mote it be."*

Place the paper in the flame. Hold the burning paper for as long as you safely can over the cauldron or cooking pot, then drop it in. The length of time it takes for the paper to burn signifies how long your wish will take to manifest. For example, if it takes only a few seconds, this corresponds to a few days, a few minutes, a few weeks, and so on. If any part of the paper doesn't burn, take that piece and repeat the spell again.

Once it has completely burned, pour the cup of wine over the paper cinders and say,

"I put myself into a position of love and trust, knowing that what I wished for shall come."

Finally, thank Bacchus for his help by drinking the glass of wine in his honor, and then say,

"Thank you, Bacchus, for all your help for my future happiness."

WISHING WELL

A SPELL CALLING ON THE POWER OF WATER
When to Perform This Spell: Any time

This is a simple wish spell that calls on the power of Cancer's element, Water, and its associated correspondences to help you to fulfill a specific wish. Remember, sometimes our wishes are simply that—wishful thinking. But if you truly believe, it will come true. As most witches say, "Be careful what you wish for!"

What You Will Need

An athame or knife

1 white candle

A small slip of paper and a pen

1 conch shell or a shell you can close

Sit calmly at your table or altar, close your eyes, and think about the wish you'd like to come true. Pick the one thing that would make the most difference in your life that is also entirely in the realm of possibility.

Now use the athame or knife to carve one or two words into the candle referring to your wish, or any symbols that you might prefer to use.

Next, light the candle and write out your wish in full on the slip of paper.

Take the conch shell in your hands and repeat your wish three times, then place the slip of paper inside the shell. Drip a few drops of candle wax onto the shell as a symbol of the wish being sealed. Blow out the candle.

Now say,

"By the power of Water my wish will come true.
By the power of this shell its work will be done.
By the power of this candle my wish will be found.
By the goddess of love and the fire of the sun
Within all that is possible, this wish will be won."

Finally, bury the conch shell under a tree or bush or place it in a box with a lid somewhere it won't be disturbed. Leave it there for two lunar cycles or until your wish comes true. If your wish doesn't come true within two lunar cycles, then you must repeat the spell.

GET WHAT YOU WANT

A SPELL CALLING ON THE MOON'S ENERGY
When to Perform This Spell: At the Full Moon

The full moon is always a time to reap rewards and finalize unfinished business. It's also a great time to focus on a goal when the moon is at its fullest, most flourishing light. This spell calls on the moon's vibrant, illuminating energy to send the tides of change working in your favor.

What You Will Need
Frankincense incense
3 pieces of red carnelian

Light your incense on your altar or a table. Place the three pieces of red carnelian (symbolizing Mars, Fire, and Aries) in a triangle shape. Now take the piece of carnelian from the top point of the triangle in your hand, close your eyes, and imagine what you want. Once you have visualized your success story in your head, open your eyes and place the carnelian back on the table. Next, pick up the piece of carnelian at the bottom right of the triangle and do the same thing, but this time as you see your desire, say,

"I believe in my intended deed,
And with this crystal, Mars, and Fire, I will succeed."

Finally, take up the last piece of carnelian and as you visualize your success, say,

"Begin my quest from this day forth and it will succeed.
And with this crystal, Mars, and Fire, my dream fulfilled."

From now on, every day for a month take the three pieces of carnelian with you wherever you go, either in a pouch or just in your pocket, to reinforce the energy you have invoked from this day and to help you to truly succeed and manifest the dream.

GET YOUR WAY

A SPELL CALLING ON BELLONA
When to Perform This Spell: Bellona's Feast (June 30)

Bellona was the ancient Roman goddess of war. You can invoke her power to fight against the odds, to get what you want, and to see the light at the end of the tunnel. Call on Bellona in the nicest possible way to avoid hurting anyone. Bellona's magic works through the placement of her magical crystals, which is the key to the success of this spell.

What You Will Need

1 piece of onyx

1 piece of carnelian

7 real pearls
(natural or cultured)

A piece of paper and a pen

1 piece of blue fluorite

First, perform the following rituals with these pieces of crystal to reinforce the spell.

Onyx brings order and enhances the ability to be mistress of your own destiny where you are no longer tied to other people's schemes. Place a piece in the north-facing corner of your bedroom to maximize self-empowerment.

Carnelian placed just inside your front door will promote confidence and build self-esteem.

Next, place seven pearls on a garden wall or in a very sunny window in your home. Make this talisman in the shape of a seven-pointed star, with the top point of the star facing south. This draws on both Bellona's power and the sun's rays. Leave for a week and then carry the pearls with you wherever you go to enhance your courage and seductive power.

With paper and pen, now write the following spell:

"Bellona, goddess wise,
I take this crystal, blue of hue
And with your blessing I shall be
As strong and wise as you and by necessity
Against all the odds I will be true."

Place this in a drawer with the piece of blue fluorite, where it will work every day to bring Bellona's influence so that you have the determination to get your way.

MANIFEST SUCCESS

A SPELL TO MAKE YOUR FUTURE SIZZLE
When to Perform This Spell: The Summanus Feast (June 28)

In ancient Rome, Summanus was the god of nocturnal thunder. He was propitiated at the end of June, when thunderstorms were particularly frequent, for a successful harvest. By invoking the thunder god's magical energy, you too can lighten your future and see clearly how to make a sizzling success of all your greatest intentions.

What You Will Need

1 white candle
2 silver-colored rings
A silver-colored box with a lid
A few drops of frankincense oil
2 white flowers

Place the magical ingredients on your table or altar and light the white candle. Put the silver rings in the box and close it. Silver is precious to Summanus and is associated with lightning. Now say,

"I call on thee, oh Summanus,
To lighten my way to brilliant times
To show me where success will be
And all who share my goals to see
The best of harvests yet to come
With this special trust we shall be done."

Sprinkle the oil onto the two white flowers and place them on top of the box. With your finger, draw an imaginary cross over the box, then an imaginary circle around the cross, to symbolize the wheel of Summanus.

Leave the box and offerings for one week, then throw the flowers away. Wear the rings every day or place in a pouch and carry them with you until the success you are looking for manifests.

MANIFEST AN ASPIRATION

A SPELL CALLING ON THE ENERGY OF THE MOON
When to Perform This Spell: A Full Moon

This full moon spell will help you with all forms of successful negotiations, particularly when you want to find compromise or be in harmony with others.

Drape the white cloth outside on a wall, garden seat, or in a tree—it must be raised above the ground for the spell to work. Place a piece of tiger's-eye (symbolizing fiery intentions and willpower) on the cloth.

What You Will Need

- 1 piece of white natural-fiber cloth (linen or cotton), about 1 square foot (30 square cm)
- 1 piece of tiger's-eye
- Fresh or dried basil leaves
- A piece of paper and a pen

Take a handful of fresh or dried basil and scatter gently over the cloth. Basil is the herb of protection and anoints the charm with protective qualities.

For a few moments, close your eyes and repeat your aspiration or desire over and over again.

Next, hold the tiger's-eye, still in the cloth, in your hand, while you vigorously shake the basil leaves to the ground. As you do so, repeat the spell:

"I am of the Universe, I flow with the cosmic sea, and wherever it will take me now, will lead me to manifest my aspiration."

Write this affirmation on a piece of paper and tuck it away in a secret place with the cloth and tiger's-eye, and by the next waxing moon your dream will manifest.

MANIFEST YOUR DREAMS

A BANISHING SPELL
When to Perform This Spell: Galungan Ceremony (December 12)

During this week-long ceremony in Bali, gods and ancestors descend to earth and good triumphs over evil. Traditionally, the Balinese use magic healing and supplications to cleanse and protect themselves from bad spirits. They also honor Vac, the goddess of charms, talismans, and speech. Invoking her magic will help you banish negativity from your life.

What You Will Need
A white sage smudging stick
A bunch of fresh flowers (whatever is in season)
Sandalwood incense
A piece of paper and a pen

First, do a simple spring cleaning of your home. This not only "cleanses" your home physically, but mentally and emotionally helps to declutter your mind, clearing the spiritual energy around you. Once you have literally cleaned up, take the bunch of sage and walk around every room of your home with the stick just smoldering. This will clear any remaining negative energy.

Next, place the flowers on your altar and say,

"Thank you, Vac, for your presence here.
In all I do, think, say, or fear
Please banish the bad and bring in the good
So that dreams be attained in the way that they should."

Next, light the incense to welcome Vac into your home, and at the table, write the following on your piece of paper in your best handwriting:

"Like Vac, I will myself announce and utter the words that gods and men alike shall welcome."

With Vac's blessing, these words will be truly magical for you.

Finally, place the paper in a safe place for the rest of the year. Now that your home and your world are safe and all negativity is banished, you can start to work on manifesting your dreams.

LOVE

Who would you like to be with?

ATTRACT LOVE AND HAPPINESS

MAKING A CORN MOTHER POPPET
When to Perform This Spell: Native American Corn Festival (July 3)

During summer, Native Americans celebrate the coming harvest by giving thanks to the Corn Mother, who represents all that is bountiful and nurturing. Some in the southeastern United States make cornhusk dolls to represent her abundance, placing them around their homes. Making your own poppet (a magic wish doll similar to a corn doll) will bring you the love and happiness you want.

You can either make a poppet by binding bundles of corn together or make one as described below, which also uses the power of magic herbs to maximize the spell's energy.

What You Will Need

A piece of paper, a pencil, and a pen

A pair of scissors

Pins, needle, and thread

Natural linen or cotton fabric

Enough dried chamomile flowers, lavender, vervain, rosemary, thyme, and mint to fill your poppet

Cinnamon or cedar incense

A bowl of dried corn kernels or rice

First, draw a rough shape of a human figure, like a gingerbread man, on a piece of paper. Cut it out and then pin it to your fabric. Use that pattern to cut two fabric gingerbread man shapes. Sew them roughly together around the edges, leaving a gap at the top of the head. Write your name and family members' names on the poppet, as well as the words "Corn Mother."

Fill and stuff the poppet with the herbs, then sew up the opening.

Light the incense and hold the poppet in the incense smoke. As you do, say,

"Mother Corn,
please bring my home good fortune now.
Bring love and happiness through this charm
To all my family send no harm.
We bless your bounty for all to see
This charm is done,
So mote it be."

Now run the fingers of your other hand through the bowl of corn or rice (representing the abundance of Earth) and repeat the charm.

Perform this entire ritual seven times (the number associated with the Corn Mother).

Keep your poppet in a secret place or put it in a powerful place where it will guard you and bring you peaceful days and happy relationships in the home.

EMPOWER YOURSELF WITH PASSION

A LOVE SPELL CALLING ON APHRODITE
When to Perform This Spell: Hallowmas (November 1)

In addition to being the goddess of love, Aphrodite was also celebrated for her ability to bring pleasure to those who gave thanks to their ancestors and the gods. Performing this spell on Hallowmas will continue Halloween's pagan celebration of souls, spirits, and ancestors. This Aphrodite love spell will bring passion into your life.

What You Will Need
5 white candles
5 pink candles
5 red candles
A conch or other seashell
A silk scarf (preferably red)
A piece of red yarn or ribbon

On your table or altar, lay out three circles of candles. Start with the white candles in the middle, then a ring of pink, and then red candles on the outer circle. Light all fifteen candles, one ring at a time, starting with the white ones. Now say:

"By the power of Aphrodite,
Bless my ritual with passion
Bless my body with desire
My lover's with more
Both entwined in love
Let this kiss be the one
That sets us on fire
So mote it be."

Now take up the shell and give it one kiss. Then say,

"By this kiss,
I bring Aphrodite's power to this spell
To wash the oceans of her love over me
To bring me passion's fire
And by this spell, so mote it be."

Place the shell in the silk scarf and tie it up with red yarn or ribbon. Set the charm in the center of the inner candle circle.

Above the flames of the candles, quickly move your hand through the air in a spiraling circle, moving your hand outward. As you do, say the charm:

"By this shell,
I call on Aphrodite
To bring me all the desire I need
So mote it be."

Once the candles have burned halfway down, blow them out, remove the silk scarf and shell, and place them under your mattress or pillow to generate true passion in your love life.

ATTRACT SOMEONE TO YOU FOR CREATIVE LOVE

A SPELL TO ENHANCE YOUR BEAUTY, FERTILITY, AND SEXUALITY
When to Perform This Spell: The Floralia (April 28)

In ancient Rome, Floralia was a pleasure-seeking festival held in honor of Flora, goddess of flowers, vegetation, and fertility. People doused themselves with perfume and decorated everything with flowers. To enhance your own beauty, fertility, and sexuality and attract someone to you for creative love, make yourself the following talisman and invoke the power of Flora into your life.

What You Will Need

A very heavy, hardback book

A bunch of your favorite flowers, or whatever is in season

Rose or orange flower/neroli eau de toilette or essential oil

Sit in a quiet place outside. Place the book and the flowers in front of you and dab the perfume on the inner side of both wrists, behind your ears, and on the outer sides of your ankles (to generate a flow of the perfume energy around you).

Take one flower from your bunch and gently pluck three petals. Place these inside the middle of the book to press for three or four weeks.

Pluck another petal and blow it from your fingers. As it lands on the ground, say,

"One for love."

Do the same with new petal and say,

"Two for desire."

Repeat with a third petal and say,

"Three for passion and fire."

Don't pick them up; just leave them where they are, and the spell is cast, even if a breeze or sudden gust of wind moves them. This is the magical natural energy of the day.

Now stand up and say,

*"Blessings, Flora, this spell is cast
Now my love must surely last."*

Take your book home and place it under a pile of heavy books or magazines. In a month's time, take out the three petals and place them in a locket or small pillbox as a charm for eternal romance with the one you love.

EMPOWER LOVE RELATIONSHIPS

AN ENCHANTMENT CALLING ON GABIJA
When to Perform This Spell: When the Sun Moves into Libra (September 22)

As the sun moves into Libra, we are thrown into the airy delights of love relationships. The goddess of Fire in Lithuanian mythology, Gabija, was worshipped by offering bread and salt and invoked to empower lovers with renewed passion. This spell will empower any love relationship with fiery energy.

What You Will Need
Frankincense incense
1 piece of pink tourmaline
Cedar oil or cedar leaves
5 red candles
5 pink candles
A chalice filled with natural spring water

Light the incense, then pass the pink tourmaline through the smoke. As you do, say:

"Gabija, goddess of fire,
Light the way to our heart's desire
Of golden sun, and lovers' power
Light the way, fill my bower
With potent magic, pure and true
And with this spell, be happy too."

Place the tourmaline crystal on your table or altar and sprinkle a little cedar oil or a few leaves over the crystal.

Place the red candles in a tight circle surrounded by the pink candles. Light all of the candles, then take the crystal in your hand and stretch it out toward the direction south and say,

"Element of Fire, pure and strong,
Bring us strength to mend all wrongs."

Now to the north say,

"Element of Earth, deep and clean,
Bring us power to manifest a dream."

Now to the west say,

"Element of Water, forever flowing,
Bring us love and passion growing."

Now to the east say,

"Element of Air, oh wise and true,
Bring us wisdom in all we do."

Next, take one of the pink candles, hold it out toward the south, and say,

"Spirit of the South, let the goddess shine her light through you."

Hold it to the north and say,

"Spirit of the North, let the goddess send her power through you."

Hold it to the east and say,

"Spirit of the East, let the goddess say her words through you."

Finally, hold it to the west and say,

"Spirit of the West, let the goddess show her love through you."

Replace the candle and take up the crystal. Place the crystal in the chalice of water and leave it for one day and one night for the magic to work.

Thank the goddess Gabija for her presence and her help, then blow out the candles.

After the one day and one night, remove the crystal from the chalice and place it in a window where it can receive maximum sunlight to continue to empower your love relationships.

IGNITE DESIRE

A SPELL TO ATTRACT SOMEONE TO YOU
When to Perform This Spell: A New Moon

Just after the new moon is the perfect time for sending out magical vibrations to create romance, beginnings, growth, and desire. This traditional European spell is one to physically attract someone to you—a stranger or someone you already know. After this spell, it will be a matter of weeks until you see results.

What You Will Need

A chalice, goblet, or wineglass

Red wine (or red grape juice)

A ring with sentimental value to you

Red thread or twine

The day after the new moon, half fill the chalice, goblet, or wineglass with the wine and take a small sip. Place it on your altar or table. Thread the ring onto the twine so you can hang it like a pendulum. Now say,

"By the power of the moon, this pendulum will ignite passion in 'His/her' (use their name) heart and soul for me."

Hold the pendulum over the glass with your elbow resting on the table. Focus on the ring and relax. Be patient as you wait for the ring to start swinging of its own accord. Once it starts to swing, focus your mind on the one you want to desire you and repeat his/her name in your head or aloud. If you don't have a name, imagine the face. If the pendulum swings linearly, then your heart's desire is thinking of you now; if the pendulum swings in a circle, then he/she will think of you tonight.

Now say,

"Moon, sun, and stars bring their love my way.
Let 'him/her' (name) find they want to stay
Each night wrapped close within my arms
Each day infatuated by my charms."

Now take the ring and the thread and wear it around your neck or carry it with you wherever you go. Repeat this spell seven days later and then another seven days later. Within that time, your lover should be thinking about you, lusting after you, and making his or her presence known.

LOVE STIRRING

A SPELL TO MAKE SOMEONE FALL IN LOVE WITH YOU
When to Perform This Spell: Eos Day (October 29)

This spell uses the power of Eos to stir love in someone's heart.

Set up the candles in a large triangle on your altar or table with the red one, representing desire and love's potency, at the apex.

Set the two white candles, which represent purity, far enough apart so that when you sit, you are almost in between.

What You Will Need

1 red candle

2 white candles

A bowl of water

Sweet incense such as rose or vanilla

1 stemmed rose

Place the bowl of water in the middle of the triangle and light the incense to the east side of the triangle, to conjure up the power of Eos and the rising sun. Then light the candles.

With the stem of the rose, stir the water in a counterclockwise direction and imagine you are stirring love in your chosen suitor's heart.

Once the water is spinning, pluck a petal from the rose and drop it into the water.

As you drop the petal, say the following enchantment so that a specific quality of your heart's desire is charged with love. For example,

"Empower his/her sense of humor with love."
"Empower his/her courage with love."
"Empower his/her kindness with love."

And so on. Continue to drop in petals for each characteristic you picture your love to have.

If the water stops spinning before you have finished describing the qualities, take the rose stem and stir again until you have listed all the qualities. When the water stops spinning, the person you described will fall in love with you.

ENFLAME A RELATIONSHIP

A CHARM CALLING ON FORTUNA
When to Perform This Spell: When the Sun Moves into Sagittarius (November 22)

If you have just begun a new relationship and want to make it sparkle with flirtatious fun and steamy sex, invoke both Fortuna's and Jupiter's luck to empower you with passion. Fortuna was the goddess of luck and fate in Roman mythology who enchanted Jupiter, took all his luck for herself, and then flew to the constellation of Sagittarius to be protected by Crotus. The magical symbol known as Laetitia, the Latin for "joy," is used to harness the power of Fortuna and her ability to bring you "joyful relating."

What You Will Need
A piece of paper and a pen
An envelope
1 piece of turquoise
1 piece of aquamarine
1 piece of calcite

First, draw the Laetitia symbol (see below) on the piece of paper and write your name and your lover's name above the top of the symbol.

Beneath the symbol, write the following:

"Oh, bountiful Fortuna, bless happiness with joy."

Fold the paper seven times and put it in an envelope. Keep it in a personal place, such as under your pillow, for seven nights to maximize the magic of luck and to invoke the power of Fortuna into your life.

On the seventh day, remove the paper and with the three crystals, place it in a window or on a table not to be disturbed. Turquoise opens you to the endless possibilities of joy in your love life, aquamarine gives you the courage to ask for your sexual needs to be met, and calcite helps you find joint pleasure in the simplest things. Make sure the point of the Laetitia symbol points to the west to attract positive, happy energy into your life, and leave for another seven days for the magic to begin to work.

START A NEW ROMANCE

A SPELL CALLING ON SELENE
When to Perform This Spell: A New Moon

If you are looking for new romance, then this spell should be cast just after the new moon to draw on the power of Selene, the moon goddess.

Place the cauldron or cooking pot on your altar between two lit pink candles. Gently drop the essential oils into the cauldron.

As you light the incense, say,

"Selene, Goddess of the moon,
Lady of enchanted light,
let love be mine and soon."

Next, tap the cauldron five times with your wand or silver spoon. Say,

"One to seek him/her,
Two to find him/her,
Three to bring him/her,
Four to bind him/her,
Heart to heart, forever one.
So with Five, this spell is done."

Tap the cauldron five more times.

Place the wand or silver spoon beside the cauldron and extinguish the candles to speed the spell upon its way.

Every evening for two weeks, repeat the words of your spell. As you do so, tap your finger five times on the rose quartz love charm you're wearing or carrying.

By the next new moon, your seductive charm will have drawn new romance to you.

What You Will Need

A cauldron or cooking pot

2 pink candles

3 drops each of essential oils of:
Rose
Lavender
Jasmine

Sandalwood incense

A wand or silver or silver-colored spoon

1 piece of rose quartz (either carry with you in your pocket or bag or wear as jewelry)

MANIFEST A NEW ROMANCE

A SPELL CALLING ON NUT
When to Perform This Spell: Any time

The ancient Egyptian sky goddess, Nut, spread her star-spangled belly across the earth at night to protect all who worshipped her. When the sun god, Ra, was trapped in the earth and couldn't ride his chariot across the sky, Nut turned into a cow that lifted him up so he could become the sun again. Exhausted, four gods rushed to Nut's aid. They later became the four winds. This wind spell honors Nut and will also help you get someone to blow a gale of kisses in your direction.

What You Will Need
9 white candles
9 red candles
9 rose petals
9 cinnamon sticks
A small bowl
Musk incense
A handful of earth
1 feather or bubbles
Water

Light the nine white candles (nine is Nut's number) and say,

"West Wind, bring new love to me.
East Wind, bring Nut's grace to me.
North Wind, let love come to me.
South Wind, send romance to me."

Light the nine red candles and call on Nut again:

"Nut, I call on you to bring his/her love for me to see."

Then take the nine red rose petals and the nine cinnamon sticks and crush them up in a small bowl with your fingers. As you do so, say the following nine times:

"Thank you, Nut, for sending the winds to blow me new love."

Now go outside and, facing south, light the stick of musk incense and for a few seconds hold it toward the south. This will ignite a stranger's passion. To the north, throw a handful of soil into the wind to manifest a lover's presence. To the east, toss a feather or blow bubbles into the wind for rapid results. And finally, to the west, sprinkle water into the wind for emotional happiness. If it is not windy, don't worry; any air that is circulating will pick up on your enchantment for the winds.

Finally, take the crushed cinnamon sticks and rose petals and bury them in a sacred or secret place. In a few weeks, your new love will be by your side.

BLESS YOUR FUTURE RELATIONSHIPS

A SPELL FOR NEW ROMANCE, MARRIAGE, AND MOVING ON
When to Perform This Spell: Gangaur Festival (April 14)

Gangaur is celebrated in Rajasthan, India, by women who worship the goddess Gauri to invoke her magic for new beginnings and marital fidelity. The women draw figures of the sun, moon, flowers, and other geometrical designs on their hands and feet. Gangaur is also worshipped by unmarried girls who believe that if they dress well for prayer, they will be granted a good husband. In this spell, get dressed up to invoke Gauri's blessing for future relationships.

What You Will Need

Your finest clothes
5 gold-colored bracelets
5 white candles
An earthenware pot
5 white flowers
Washable face paint or pens you can use on your skin

First, dress in your finest clothes and wear your precious jewelry. As you do so, stare in the mirror and tell yourself that you are going to have the most spectacular marriage, new romance, or new beginning ever.

Place the five golden bracelets in a circle on the table or your altar and place the five white candles in the center of each bangle. Now place the earthenware pot in the middle of the circle and the white flowers inside. (These represent the treasures of Gauri.)

Light the candles, and as they burn and flicker, draw on the top of your left foot the symbol of the sun (a circle with a dot in the middle) and on your right foot the symbol of the moon (a crescent moon).

Next, repeat the following invocation to draw on Gauri's powers.

"Oh, Gauri, let this happiness be mine.
It can't be changed by wiles or rue.
With your help and magic true
By sun and moon, and all the stars
This spell brings fresh starts all anew."

Repeat this five times (Gauri's magic number), and for each chant, draw another sun and moon on your feet, until you have a total of five suns and five moons.

When you have performed the ritual, blow out the candles and keep the symbols on your feet for at least twenty-four hours for the magic to work.

BIND A RELATIONSHIP

A SPELL USING YIN AND YANG
When to Perform This Spell: Chongyang Festival (In the first 3 weeks of October, actual date changes yearly)

In the ancient Taoist magical text known as the *I Ching*, the number 9 symbolized yang (potent masculine energy). *Chong* in Chinese means "double," or the number 2, and represents yin, (receptive feminine energy). So the Chongyang festival, or the Double Ninth Festival, celebrates the union of opposites. By drawing on the power of numbers and the combined power of feminine and male energies in this spell, any long-term love relationship will be blessed and harmonized. The rings here symbolize this power: silver to represent yin (feminine) and gold to represent yang (masculine).

What You Will Need

2 rings (1 silver colored, 1 gold colored. However, real gold and silver are imbued with divine power and will maximize the power of the spell.)

Silken thread or ribbon

A pouch or bag made of silk or cotton

A small box with a lid or an envelope

1 white candle (for purity)

1 red candle (for passion)

Tie the rings together with a silken thread or ribbon. Natural fabrics, such as gold and silver, are further imbued with divine energy.

Place the rings on your window ledge for three nights to amplify the power threefold by the light of the moon. Even if you can't see the moon, it is still working its magic.

Next, place your moon-enriched rings into the pouch or bag and place it under your pillow for four nights. Remove the pouch the next morning and carry it wherever you go for five days.

Remove the rings from the pouch and place on the window ledge for six more days. Carry it with you again on the seventh, eighth, and ninth days.

On the ninth day, take the rings out of the pouch and seal them in a box or envelope. Place this in a drawer or special place forever.

On the tenth day, light the two candles, close your eyes, and affirm the following:

"We are bound together forever, each in the other, as yin and yang are one."

From now on, you will be in harmony with your beloved.

ATTRACT BETTER SEX

A CHARM WITH A HORSESHOE
When to Perform This Spell: A New Moon

This charm uses the power of the lucky horseshoe, which is associated with virility. It was used among French country folk during the fifteenth century as a talisman to restore the sex drives of weary soldiers returning home from the wars.

Place the horseshoe—with the curve at the bottom—on your altar or table. Bless the shoe with the oils by simply wiping a little of each fragrance onto the horseshoe.

What You Will Need

A horseshoe

Tuberose perfume or essential oil

Gardenia perfume or essential oil

Jasmine perfume or essential oil

Red and blue silk threads

2 nails or 2 screws

As you do so, say,

"By the anointing of this shoe
Soon my love will be perfumed
With virile spice and passion high.
No one can stop our love's desire."

Next, wind the red and blue threads (representing male and female power, respectively) around the horseshoe. Make three knots to hold them in place, and each time you make a knot, whisper to yourself what your greatest sexual secret desire is.

Hold the shoe in your hands, close to your heart, and say,

"By the holding of this shoe
The power of desire takes over too.
We will not stop from dusk till dawn
With lovers' heat and sex reborn."

Use the nails or screws to hang the horseshoe above your bedroom door with the opening of the shoe to the top. From now on, your love life will be blessed with pure passion and fulfilling sex.

GET IN TOUCH WITH YOUR SEXUAL NEEDS

A SPELL FOR PERFECT SEXUAL HARMONY
When to Perform This Spell: Beltane (May 1)

The May Day celebration of dancing around the maypole is part of the Celtic fertility celebration known as Beltane. Traditionally, Beltane began when the hawthorn tree, also known as the May tree, blossomed. The tree of sexuality and fertility, its flower is also used as decoration. This spell draws on the powers of the May god and goddess to increase your seductive powers tenfold and put you in touch with your true sexual needs.

What You Will Need
A piece of paper
A pen or pencil
A box with a lid
7 pieces of red garnet
7 white candles
Sprigs of hawthorn blossom, or if unavailable, an image of hawthorn blossom

Draw a symbol of the sun (circle with a dot in the center) at the top of the paper and a symbol of the moon (crescent moon) at the bottom of the paper, to represent the union of the Green Man and the May goddess, Flora. In the middle of the paper, draw a large circle and within the circle write:

"By the power of the God and Goddess twice
We are united, in love, in physical embrace
And in our sexuality."

Fold the paper four times and place it in your special box. This will disperse all negative energy around you, so that you and your lover are ready for perfect sexual harmony. Close the lid and place in a south-facing window to maximize the power of Flora and the Green Man.

In the southeast corner of your bedroom, place one piece of garnet to inspire romance and passionate love. Place another garnet under your pillow to ignite intimacy and place the remaining five pieces on your table or altar in a circle.

Light the seven white candles, placing three on either side of the circle and the seventh in the middle. Gaze into the flame of the middle candle, concentrate on your lover or intended one, and say:

"By the power of the Sacred Marriage
I anoint true love with this sacred wine
For sexual potency and desire
Will be all yours, and mine."

Now place the hawthorn blossom on top of your box. Leave the garnets in place for as long as you desire. Remove the hawthorn blossom before the next evening and bury it under a tree or bush (or even in a flowerpot) for the magic of the goddess and Green Man to improve your sex life.

BEGUILE AND BEWITCH

AN ENCHANTMENT TO SEDUCE
When to Cast This Spell: Feast of Meditrina (October 11)

Legend tells of how Roman goddess of wine Meditrina once, just before sunset, made an aphrodisiac from wine, cloves, and nutmeg. She offered it to the sun god, Sol, seducing him into taking her on his golden chariot as it raced toward the night sky. Harness Meditrina's seductive powers by taking one sip of her magic potion while you petition her help. It is best to cast your spell just before sunset.

Make a small circle of twelve pebbles, stones, or quartz crystals on the floor, or outside where the sunset energy is more intense. These stones represent the twelve constellations through which Sol travels at night.

What You Will Need

- 12 pebbles, stones, or white quartz crystals
- A metal cup or bowl (preferably gold- or silver-plate, pewter, or copper)
- 4 white candles
- A handful of red rose petals
- 3 cloves
- A glass of red wine or grape juice

Place the metal bowl or cup in the center of the circle and sit or kneel before the circle facing west, the direction of the setting sun.

Place and light the four white candles to the west, north, east, and south of the bowl, in that order, to invoke the energy of the elements Water, Earth, Air, and Fire, which rule these directions respectively.

Close your eyes and gently focus in your mind on the qualities or image of the one you want to seduce. Do this for approximately three minutes.

Take the rose petals, which represent desire, and the three cloves—to symbolize love, harmony, and togetherness—and place them in the vessel.

Take one sip of wine and pour the rest into your cup or bowl. As you do so, affirm to yourself:

"Bless me, Meditrina, burning true and gold
With power to take Sol round the world
Bless me with power to court and woo
And take what's mine both right and true."

Let the candles burn on while you focus again for three minutes on the one you want to seduce. Now blow the candles out. Thank Meditrina for her blessing and leave your enchantment in place overnight.

For the following week, you will be able to seduce anyone you choose.

SEDUCE SOMEONE

A LOVE SPELL CALLING ON ARIADNE
When to Perform This Spell: Halloween (October 31)

In the ancient palaces of Minoan Crete, serpent goddess–worshipping high priestesses enchanted wealthy traders and seafarers, often using locally grown saffron. It is believed that Ariadne, the original serpent goddess notorious for giving Theseus a thread to find his way out of the labyrinth, guarded the secret of saffron magic. According to legend, if any stranger appeared on the day of the year devoted to the ghosts of ancestors (known today as Halloween), he had to prove to the serpent goddess that he was a virile man. This love spell was used by the priestesses.

What You Will Need

1 bright red or orange candle

3 saffron threads

A bowl of sea salt

A glass of clear pure spring water

A spicy incense stick such as cinnamon, myrrh, or frankincense

Place the candle on a table or altar and place the saffron, salt, and water beside it. Light the candle, and say,

"Oh, lady Ariadne, give me the power to seduce and the reward of my desire."

Now light the incense and let it burn until it is smoking.

Sprinkle the sea salt around the candle, and as you do so, say,

"Bring me my heart's desire, Oh sacred Earth."

Next, pass your hand in the air around the candle and say,

"Bring me my heart's desire, Oh sacred Fire."

Next, pass your hand through the smoke of the incense and say,

"Bring me my heart's desire, Oh sacred Air."

Drop the saffron into the water and say,

"Bring me my heart's desire, Oh sacred Water."

Next, touch the surface of the water and say the following:

*"Oh, Ariadne, let desire be mine
And with this spell, desire be theirs
For me alone, but none to bind."*

Now place your finger through the incense smoke and repeat the words of the spell.

To release the energy, say,

*"Ariadne, thank you for bringing me desire, seductive skills, and new love to my
door. So mote it be."*

Finally, snuff out the candle and incense, remove the threads of saffron from the water, and lay them on your altar. When dry, carefully place them in an envelope and keep them in a safe place to activate your seductive powers for the next three months.

INVOKE SEDUCTIVE CHARMS

A VITALITY CHARM
When to Perform This Spell: Day of Frigga (November 27)

Frigga, known as the beloved lady, was the consort of the mythical Norse god Odin, and she represents feminine power and outer beauty. She was known to carry a box of secret potions that turned ugly mortals into beautiful nymphs. With Frigga's magic vitality box, you can contain, invoke, capture, and exude all forms of seductive charms, be vitalized, and love yourself at all times.

On a piece of paper, write a list of all the qualities you aspire to, or what would make you feel beautiful, loved, or just good to be you.

What You Will Need

A piece of paper and a pen

A small shallow box with a lid, such as a shoe box

A photo of yourself you truly like

1 white quartz crystal

Twigs of wood (preferably hazel or hawthorn)

1 acorn or oak leaf (or the image of one)

5 rose petals

Next, on the lid of the box, draw a triple moon symbol (see right) to represent Frigga's powers. Inside your paper wish list, place the photo of yourself, the white quartz, the twigs, and the acorn or oak leaf. Place the rose petals on top of the photo and close the lid. As you do, say,

"Oh, goddess Frigga,
Please bless this box of twigs
With beauty pure indeed
So I can be the best of myself
For all that I shall need."

Now place the box in a secret place. Whenever you want to draw on Frigga's beauty for yourself or feel good to be you, take out the box and repeat the following:

"The dreams that lie within the earth awaken now.
The beauty in me will awaken now.
The stars await as so do I.
Grow true, grow strong, toward the sky."

Each time you open the box, take out the white quartz crystal, hold it in your hand, and repeat the spell above to maximize and embrace Frigga's beneficial help. You will be revitalized and ready for every opportunity or challenge that comes your way.

KEEP A LOVER FROM STRAYING

A LOVE CHARM
When to Perform This Spell: The Day After a New Moon

Sometimes we believe our love will leave us, but this spell, without doing any harm to your beloved, will activate his or her desire to stay put. You must do this spell only on the day after the new moon.

What You Will Need

A piece of paper and a pen
A few basil leaves
1 piece of amber
A pouch

Draw a pentagram (see page 19) on the paper and then in each of the five star points, write your name. In the center, write your lover's name.

Wrap the paper around the basil and amber and place all the ingredients into a pouch. Take it to a river, stream, lake, or pond (or use a bowl of spring water, if you can't). Dip the pouch into the water, without letting go, and say the charm,

"Thank you, goddess of the moon,
Fulfill my desire and let it be.
Direct his/her love only to me.
This is my will, so mote it be."

Take the pouch out of the water and now bury it somewhere secret and safe. Leave it there until you know, deep in your heart, that your love will be true to you forever.

CHANGE SOMEONE'S HEART

A MAGIC RING AND LOVE SPELL
When to Perform This Spell: Saint Valentine's Day (February 14)

Christian martyr Saint Valentine healed his jailer's daughter and, just before his execution, sent her a letter that read, "Farewell, from your Valentine." By the medieval period, the day became associated with romance and spells were cast to ensure success in love. Magic rings have been used since then to attract love, often entwined with either the hair of the loved one or a red ribbon. For the spell to work, you must never tell that person about the talisman.

First, write the name of the one whose feelings you want to change on the piece of paper with the silver pen.

Take the ring and twine the red ribbon or thread around it until the ring is covered.

As you do so, say,

"Thrice I bind, thrice times their love for me.
Thrice I bind and thrice times thrice their ecstasy.
For with this charm they will be mine.
Not bound, but free to love in chosen time."

What You Will Need

A piece of black paper and a silver pen

A simple silver or silver-colored ring or band with no markings. (It doesn't have to fit your finger, because this is one ring you won't be wearing on your hand.)

2 lengths of red silk ribbon or thread

2 bay leaves

1 willow leaf

1 rowan tree leaf (if not available, 1 piece of rose quartz)

A glass or glass bowl filled with rosewater

Gently drop the leaves and the ring into the bowl of rosewater. Place the paper in a window, on a ledge or table nearby, to be activated by the moon.

Place the bowl of water with the ring and other ingredients upon the paper. The following evening, remove the ring. Wait for the ribbon to dry even if it takes a day or so, then thread the ring—still bound by the ribbon—onto another piece of silk cord. Wear it around your neck and say,

"Thank you, Venus, for this gift.
My love will turn, the change will be,
My love will see, then love will turn,
A heart will change and come to me."

Wear the ring for three more days or keep it in a pouch and carry it with you. The spell will invoke change in someone's heart, or someone will see you in a new and beautiful light.

KEEP OTHERS' EYES OFF YOUR LOVER

A LOVE SPELL CALLING ON MELUSINE
When to Perform This Spell: Any time

To prevent your lover's eyes from wandering, cast a spell that will repel all other love interests. This spell invokes the power of the cursed water nymph Melusine, who medieval legend tells was transformed into a serpent. Only a knight's kiss would make her beautiful again. But each knight who saw her was repelled by her serpent form, so she cast a spell on them all so that none would ever be loved.

What You Will Need

1 green candle

A photo of your lover, or you can just write his/her name on a piece of paper

1 piece of amber

1 sprig of basil

A pouch

For all the spells in this book to work, belief is essential. So believe, believe, and thrice believe what you are saying during the spell, and with that kind of intention, things that you want to happen will happen.

Light the green candle, and while holding the image or name of your lover, chant these words:

"I call upon the powers of Melusine's attraction
To now work in reverse,
To repel all others
From my lover's eyes
No longer to be cursed."

Blow out the candle and then place the amber and the basil in the pouch at a window for one night, beside the name or photo of your lover. Soon your lover will only have eyes for you.

BANISH UNWANTED ATTENTION

A SPELL TO DISSUADE YOUR ADMIRER
When to Perform This Spell: Any time

Rather like using a charm to ward off the evil eye, this simple enchantment will stop your unwanted admirer in his or her tracks. However, you must truly be gentle when doing this spell, because if you have any resentment or malice in your heart . . . remember, what goes around comes around.

What You Will Need
A piece of paper and a pen
1 black candle
1 piece of black obsidian

On the piece of paper, write a list of the positive attributes of the person you want to deter, such as his or her job, home, or leisure pursuits—write whatever comes to mind, so long as what you write is not negative.

Next, light your black candle and sit quietly before the flame as you repeat this enchantment seven times:

"The Stars above, the Stone below
Extinguish these flames of love right now.
With Earth it rises o'er our heads
With Air it empties both our beds.
With Water, gold and Vitriol
We will be parted forever so.
Great Heavens, Stars, and Oceans pure
Take away unwanted desire
To never come to me again
And then this spiral flame will end."

Finally wrap the paper around the black obsidian stone and bury it in the garden or somewhere outside where no one can find it. As you bury it, say,

"Thus ends this infatuation so mote it be."

You will be free from the attention of the one you do not want in your life by the next full moon.

BREAK AN INFATUATION

A SPELL CALLING ON EOS
When to Perform This Spell: Eos Eve (October 28)

Eos, Greek goddess of the dawn, was cursed by Aphrodite to eternally fall in love with mortals. Eos represents the universal energy that flows through all things. As she rises every morning, she hopes one day that by helping others, her own curse will be broken. To break an infatuation, either yours or someone else's for you, you need to draw on the power of Eos and her life force.

What You Will Need
You

Go for a walk outside, preferably alone, as early in the day and as near to sunrise as you can to draw on the full power of Eos.

As you walk, step slowly and look at the ground beneath you. When you see stones, pebbles, shells, or any natural objects that appeal to you, pick them up. They should be small enough to carry in your pocket or a small bag.

Each time you pick up a stone, hold it and feel its natural power permeating your skin, filling you with inspiration and spiritual power.

When you have seven stones (the number seven connects us to magical or divine forces), sit down in a comfortable place and put the stones in your lap. Close your eyes and concentrate on the person you want to banish from your life, but without intending them any harm.

Remove one stone from your lap and throw it as far away from you as possible as you say:

"Eos, release me from the infatuation by tomorrow's dawn."

Throw second stone far from you in any direction, and say,

"Eos, release me from the infatuation by the second dawn."

With the third stone, say,

"Eos, release me from the infatuation by the third dawn."

Continue until you have thrown all seven stones, counting each one as another dawn. When you have finished, put your hands together in prayer and thank Eos for helping to release you from your love addiction.

Within seven dawns, this spell will work its magic and either you or someone else will no longer be bound by infatuation.

GET YOUR EX BACK

A LOVE SPELL
When to Perform This Spell: Midsummer's Day/Solstice (June 20–22)

Midsummer's Day is the only day in the year when this spell will work. You can pick out your locations beforehand, but you must place the roses, which represent true love, on Midsummer's Day.

Bury one rose under the fruit tree, which represents the element Earth. Place another near the gate of the church, to represent the element Air; another near running water, to represent the element Water; and another one beside a crossroads, at the south corner, or whichever of the corners is nearest the south, to doubly enhance the power of Fire, the element which harnesses passion.

The last rose goes under your own pillow.

Sleep with the rose under your pillow.

On the following day, pluck the petals from that rose and say,

"This power of love reach out and beyond
Of water, of earth, of air, and of fire.
Midsummer nymphs take my lover this light
To bring him back from this magical round
By his own will and desire, he will want to be mine."

Now, return to the four locations where you left the roses. Pluck three petals (to represent the union of two plus the power of love) from each rose at each location and scatter them at each location. Your ex will be back very soon, if you truly believe that your spell will work.

What You Will Need

5 red roses

A fruit tree

A church

Natural moving water, like a stream, river, or the sea

A crossroads

GET OVER A BREAKUP

A CHARM CALLING ON SATURN
When to Perform This Spell: Any time

To get over rejection, a breakup in a relationship, or a parting of the ways whether personal or business, you can invoke the power of Saturn's strength and resolve and free yourself from the attachment.

Draw the two magical symbols for regaining loss, known as Amissio (see left), on two different pieces of paper. Then turn two cups upside down over the symbols, leave for six days (Saturn's magical number), remove, and burn in your cauldron or cooking pot. This will harness the powers of the god Saturn to bring you inner strength.

What You Will Need
2 pieces of paper and a pen
2 chalices or cups
A cauldron or cooking pot
6 pieces of amazonite or moss agate crystal

After six days, place six pieces of amazonite or moss agate in your garden or somewhere outside where they won't be disturbed, in the shape of the Amissio symbol. Every day for four days, turn each stone 90 degrees in a clockwise direction, until on the fourth day they're in their original position. This reinforces the magical powers of Saturn's symbol Amissio to work in your favor and bring you renewed self-esteem, value, and the confidence to move on.

HOME AND FAMILY

How would you like to live?

ENCOURAGE FERTILITY

A SPELL TO BRING CREATIVE AND FERTILE REWARDS
When to Perform This Spell: Matronalia (March 1)

The Matronalia was an ancient Roman festival celebrating the goddess Juno as protector of childbirth, motherhood, and women. Roman women received gifts from husbands, spells for fertility and childbirth were cast, and wealthier women gave their slaves a day off. This spell will invoke the power of fertility deities and bring you good luck for childbirth, fertility, and mind-body creativity.

What You Will Need
A piece of paper and a pen
1 piece of rose quartz
5 pieces of moonstone

On the morning of March 1st, draw the Puella symbol (see right) on a piece of paper by making four large dots in a diamond shape, with a fifth dot underneath the fourth. Write your name above the top point and beneath the symbol write what you want to manifest successfully (for example, "pregnancy," "fertility," "good childbirth," "creative inspiration"). Place a piece of rose quartz on the symbol for twenty-four hours to activate the energy and to vibrate with your personal world.

After twenty-four hours, place the rose quartz under your pillow and keep it there until a waxing moon, when you should move it to the windowsill so that your fertility energy is magnified by the moon's influence. After the full moon, place it back under your pillow for two more weeks so that your female hormones, creative ideas, and childbearing ability are imbued with this ritual energy.

Also on March 1st, arrange five pieces of moonstone in the symbol of Puella, preferably outside, with the top of the symbol pointing westward. This will reinforce the rose quartz ritual and help to harness mother earth's fertility and feminine power. Within two lunar cycles, your wishes will be fulfilled. If you are pregnant and not due within these next eight weeks, repeat the spell two weeks before your due date for a happy childbirth.

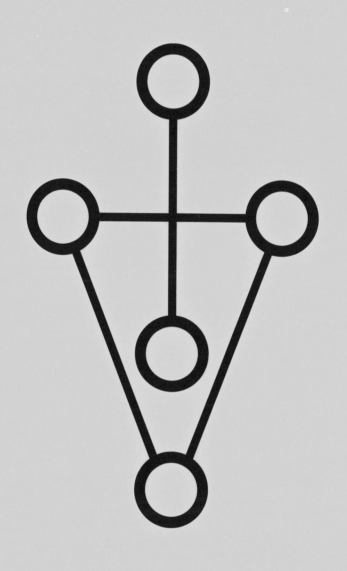

CLEANSE AND CALM YOUR HOME

A Spell Calling on Neptune
When to Perform This Spell: Neptunalia (July 20)

In mid-July, typically a time of drought, the Romans appeased and worshipped Neptune, god of the seas. They built huts from branches and leaves in which to feast, drink, and make merry. Rituals were performed to purify the home with Neptune's sacred waters. This charm uses the powers of Neptune, Jupiter, Saturn, and Mercury to calm the energy in your home.

What You Will Need

Frankincense incense
1 white candle
A bowl or dish of salt
A bowl of clean, pure water

Light the incense and the candle. Stand before your altar or table and take a few moments to feel at one with the energies of your home. Notice the smells, the sounds, the breeze moving the curtains, or the sunlight entering your room.

When you are ready, say:

"I charge you Saturn, Mercury, Jupiter, Neptune,
To sweep my house clean of all ill and bane.
This is my will, so mote it be."

Take the dish of salt and, working clockwise around the house, throw a pinch of salt into each corner of every room, saying:

"By the powers of Saturn, I cleanse this house."

Using the same route you used with the salt, take the incense through the house and say,

"By the powers of Mercury, I cleanse this house."

Do the same with the candle and say,

"By the powers of Jupiter, I cleanse this house."

With the bowl of water, sprinkle water throughout the house, in every corner and at all exits and entrances, and say,

"By the powers of Neptune, I cleanse this house."

Set the bowl on the table and stand for a few minutes in silence. Your home will feel calmer and more peaceful, fresh, and clean. Let the candle burn down until you need to snuff it out, and just before you do so, sprinkle salt and then water on the flames to evoke the powers of all the gods.

CLEARING NEGATIVITY

A SPELL CALLING ON THE LADY OF CARMEL
When to Perform This Spell: Any time

The early Carmelite monks were Christian hermits who lived on Mount Carmel in the Holy Land during the late Middle Ages. They built a chapel dedicated to the Blessed Virgin, who they called the Lady of the Place. Whatever spiritual practice you follow, the Lady of Carmel will bring balance of mind, spirit, and soul to your home and family.

Start by repeating the following psychic healing affirmations five times.

1. My spiritual self will stay with me even when I am being pragmatic.

2. Love is all around me; I know it is there to benefit me.

3. I believe in the life force that heals all.

4. The power of belief is mine to give to others and to myself.

What You Will Need

Sandalwood incense or a smudging stick of white sage

A small piece of paper

A pen and black ink

A small pouch or bag made of black velvet or silk

1 small white quartz crystal

1 pinch of dried sage

1 pinch of dried wormwood

1 silver-colored coin

1 strand of your hair

1 piece of raffia or twine

When you are ready, use a small bundle of dried white sage or sandalwood incense to "smudge" or cleanse negative energy from your home. Light the sage or incense and walk from room to room, taking your time to fill each room with smoke. In each room say:

"All negative energy be gone, all negative energy be gone, thank you, Lady of the Place."

Next, draw a pentagram (page 19) in black ink on a small piece of paper. Roll the paper and place it in the black pouch or bag.

Also place in the pouch the white quartz crystal (Fire), a pinch of sage (Air), a pinch of wormwood (Earth), the silver coin (Water), and a strand of your hair.

Tie the bag up with some raffia or twine using three knots. As you tie each knot, say:

*"As My Lady's spell is done
So my home be ever loved
My spirit self in harmony
With all I do or think or be."*

Place the knotted pouch on a window ledge for one lunar cycle to ensure spiritual, mental, and emotional harmony.

ENSURE FAMILY LUCK AND HAPPINESS

An Enchantment Calling on the Three Graces
When to Perform This Spell: Any time

This general spell will bring you beneficial energy in and around the home, as well as improve relationships with family members. With the help of the triple Greek goddess in the guise of three Graces—Aglaea (Splendor), Euphrosyne (Mirth), and Thalia (Good Cheer)—you can also make your home a lucky place to live. The twelve ingredients used represent the astrological signs and invoke attributes of the powers of the three Graces.

What You Will Need

Yellow rosebuds (or 3 images of yellow rosebuds)

3 garlic cloves

3 gold-colored coins

3 gold-colored rings

A small bag or pouch

Gold ribbon

1 iron nail

Place the rosebuds, garlic, coins, and rings in the bag and tie it up with the gold ribbon. Take the bag and walk around your home in a clockwise direction, starting at the outer perimeter and holding the bag in front of you. Cover every part of your home and gradually work your way into a center point. As you walk, repeat the following charm,

"Thrice times I walk to honor my home.
Three Graces help me wherever I roam
To bring me luck in all I do
My family too, with help from you."

Now make the same walk, but in a counterclockwise direction, repeating the charm below:

"This magic pouch holds virtues sweet
Each zodiac sign, each element writ
With love and luck sealed in its place
It's time to thank you all for Grace."

Finally take your pouch and hang it over your front door using an iron nail, which has the magical property of fixing all that you desire in place in the home. Your home will be blessed with luck for months to come.

ATTRACT GOOD VIBRATIONS

A Spell Calling on Athena
When to Perform This Spell: A New Moon

Athena, the Greek goddess of wisdom, courage, inspiration, and a whole lot more was also the patroness of weaving. This weaving spell calls on Athena's help to weave love and wisdom into your home and to bring peace and harmony. The ingredients are all colors and fabrics associated with Athena's elements, Fire and Air.

First, lay out the white cloth on your altar, table, or somewhere you will be able to leave it for three days without the spell being disturbed.

What You Will Need

A white cloth made of silk, cotton, or linen, about 2 feet (60 cm) long and 1 foot (30 cm) wide

3 red candles

3 yellow candles

3 red silk ribbons, about 2 feet (60 cm) long

3 yellow velvet ribbons, about 2 feet (60 cm) long

Place the three red candles to the left of the cloth and the three yellow candles to the right.

Take one red ribbon and two yellow ribbons, tie a knot at one end, braid them until you get to the other, and tie a second knot. Lay the braid along the length of the cloth, then do the same with the two red ribbons and the remaining yellow ribbon.

Now light the candles and say,

"I call on you, Athena, to be my guide today
To help me weave blessing and harmony
Upon my home, always."

Take one woven braid in each hand, and hold them up in the air above the cloth (do not let them get singed by the candles).

As you hold them, say,

"With woven ribbons my home is safe
With woven threads comes love and peace
With woven colors yellow and red
I now invoke Athena's grace
To make this home the perfect place."

Finally, blow out the candles, then place the braided ribbons back on the altar cloth for three days and three nights to bring Athena's harmonious influence to your home.

BRING YOUR HOME PEACE AND HAPPINESS

An Enchantment Calling on Eirene
When to Perform This Spell: Eirene's Hour (December 25)

Eirene, goddess of peace, was depicted in art carrying a horn overflowing with fruits and flowers. One of the three Horai, the goddesses of the seasons and the keepers of the gates of heaven, Eirene also personified one of the Nine Hours of the day between sunrise and sunset. The word hora means "the correct moment," so perform this spell during Eirene's "hour" between 1 p.m. and 2 p.m., to align with her correct moment and bring you a happy future.

At precisely 1 p.m., fill your horn with the various fruits and herbs. Place carefully on your altar or on a table as an offering to Eirene.

Next, on a piece of paper, draw the glyph for the sun (a circle with a dot in the center) on one side and the glyph for Jupiter on the other side (see right). Fold it carefully four times and place it on your altar or sacred space next to the horn of plenty. Now say,

"For peace and wealth, bring me thy skill,
Within this talisman luck instill
That I may fare successfully,
As I will, so mote it be."

Leave your horn of plenty and the paper charm to Eirene until the clock strikes 2 p.m. and then remove it from the table or altar. Take the paper talisman and place it in a drawer in your desk or keep it with you in your handbag if you are traveling throughout the day, to ensure peace and happiness for the new year.

What You Will Need

A horn of plenty. (This can be a horn-shaped drinking vessel or bowl, or you can make a replica by twisting a conical shape out of stiff paper and then stapling the edges to keep it in shape.)

3 fruits (a pomegranate, a fig, an apple, or grapes are best)

Rose petals

1 sprig of lavender (or pinch of dried lavender)

A piece of paper and a pen

RECONCILE WITH SOMEONE

A Spell for Reconciliation and Reunions
When to Perform This Spell: The Tanabata (July 7)

The Japanese star festival Tanabata celebrates the long-awaited reunion of Orihime and Hikoboshi, deities separated the rest of the year by the Milky Way and represented by the stars Vega and Altair, respectively. In present-day Japan, people write wishes on pieces of paper and hang them on bamboo sticks that are often set afloat on a river or burned. A magical verse associated with this festival, translated into English here, invokes togetherness and the coming together of family members.

What You Will Need

A pen or a pencil

5 strips of different-colored paper

1 gold-colored chain necklace

1 silver-colored chain necklace

On each strip of paper, write down one wish that includes some form of happy reunion, reconciliation, or just a better way of relating between you and your loved ones.

Place the gold and silver chains, representing Altair and Vega, respectively, on your table or altar in circle shapes and then place the five wishes in a bundle across the chains.

Calm your mind and concentrate on the magical ingredients on the table and your wishes.

Then say the following charm:

"The stars twinkle
On the gold and silver grains of sand.
The five-color paper strips
I have already written.
The stars twinkle,
they watch us from heaven.
Thank you, Altair and Vega, for your blessing."

The following evening, tear up the paper wishes and place the scraps under a tree or bush, or throw them into a stream or river—or anywhere outside where no one can find them—so the magic of the stars, Altair and Vega, may activate your wishes to come true.

REPAIR A FRIENDSHIP

A Friendship Repair Charm
When to Perform This Spell: A New Moon and a Full Moon

Make up with a friend or repair any rift by calling on the goddess Artemis, whose wise counsel as arbitrator was employed by the gods. The spell works in two parts. You must perform the first part just after the new moon, and the second part at the full moon.

What You Will Need

1 piece of turquoise
1 pink candle
Vanilla extract or essential oil
A piece of paper and a pen

Place the piece of turquoise and the candle at your altar or your table.

Gently rub the vanilla extract on the sides of the candle and then light it. Ask Artemis to join you by saying,

"With perfumed oil and candle fair
Welcome, Artemis, to this my lair
Where treasured friends can be again
Within one lunar cycle our rift to mend
The bond repaired, the wounds all healed
Our friendship blessed with your appeal."

Sit for a few minutes in quiet contemplation of your friendship and the happy times you shared. When you feel full of love for your pal, write down all the things you like or admire about your friend. Blow out the candle, fold the paper, and place it in a drawer with the piece of turquoise.

On the eve of the full moon, relight the candle and retrieve the list and the turquoise. Holding the turquoise in your hand, read the list aloud. Then say,

"Had I but silver and gold,
I would weave a charm of destiny
For you and I to be entwined in friendship ever bound.
In this my heart is true and found
The spell now every day be wound
Around our hearts forever.
With perfumed oil and candle fair
Thank you, Artemis, for this day true
Where treasured friends can be again
By my side within day one.
The bond repaired, the wounds all healed
Our friendship blessed with your appeal."

Bow to the candle, then gently blow it out as if blowing a kiss to your friend. Arrange to meet your friend and take the turquoise with you to present as a peace offering.

CAREER

What would you like to become?

START A NEW PROJECT

AN ENCHANTMENT FOR STARTING NEW ENTERPRISES
When to Perform This Spell: Eve of Beltane (April 30)

In pagan Europe, the beginning of the pastoral summer season was marked by Beltane, when nature spirits were thought to be especially active. The symbol of fire was used to benefit growth and to call on the spirits of nature and the waxing power of the sun to bring a creative beginning to the season. On the eve of Beltane, harness those same spirits and energy to benefit you in any new enterprise or creative endeavor.

What You Will Need

A large piece of paper and a pen

A cauldron or cooking pot

5 twigs, preferably from 5 different species of trees: oak, rowan, elder, hazel, and willow. (If you can't find them, take photos or images of them from a book or the Internet and paste them onto separate pieces of paper.

On your main piece of paper, draw a pentacle: a five-pointed star within a circle, with the fifth point to the north or top of the circle.

Write the magic elemental words between each of the points as follows:

To left of the top point, *"Spirit."*

To the right of the top point, *"Air."*

Above the bottom right point, *"Fire."*

Between the two bottom points, *"Earth."*

Above the bottom left point, *"Water."*

Now place the five twigs into the cauldron or cooking pot and with an imaginary wand encircle the cauldron five times and say,

"Five woods into the Cauldron go
Burn them fast and burn them slow.
When the wheel begins to turn
Soon the Beltane fires will burn.
Where the rippling waters go
Cast a stone, the truth you'll know.
These Eight words the Rede fulfill
'An Ye Harm None, Do What Ye Will.'"

The spirits of the woods, trees, and waters will now be there to help you activate any new enterprise in the coming months.

FOR PROSPEROUS BEGINNINGS

ENCHANTMENT TO BENEFIT ANY NEW PROJECTS
When to Perform This Spell: Songkran Festival (April 13)

It is said that Brahma lost his head to Phra-In, the god of wealth and king of the gods. The head was given to seven goddesses. Their passing it from one to the next signaled the start of the new year, today celebrated with the Songkran festival, during which Thai people throw water at each other. Though Phra-In's appearance at the festival indicates future weather trends, his magic will help you achieve a fresh start in business or lifestyle, financial benefits, prosperous living, good luck, and blessings.

What You Will Need

A bowl of spring water
A bowl of rice
A bowl of your favorite fruit
1 piece of green tourmaline

To honor Phra-In, first sprinkle some of the spring water all around the floors of your home. It should be just enough to seem like gentle rain, the kind you would imagine being right for a good harvest. If you have outside space, do the same outside too; this invokes the rain god.

At the entrance to your home, place the bowl of rice (a symbol of happiness), the bowl of fruit (symbolizes the element Earth), and the piece of green tourmaline (enhances vitality and courage). Leave them all day as an offering of welcome to the prosperity and wealth of Phra-In. In the evening, remove your offerings and place the green tourmaline under your pillow for the night.

The god's magic will begin to work into your life over the next few days; the longer you leave the green tourmaline beneath your pillow, the more powerful the magic and the better the results.

CHANGE CAREERS

ENCHANTMENT FOR CAREER CHANGE
When to Perform This Spell: Blossom Festival (February 25)

Hanami, meaning "flower viewing," is a Japanese tradition of celebrating the transient beauty of the cherry and plum blossom. In ancient Japan, families would picnic under the cherry blossom trees as a celebration of spring. As a symbol of rebirth and the fleeting nature of the blossom, its magic is harnessed to enjoy future change in career and vocation.

Before you start, imagine and think clearly about what kinds of things make you feel joyful.

What You Will Need
- 1 white candle
- 3 twigs of cherry or plum blossoms in flower, (If not available, use an image, illustration, photo, or painting of cherry or plum blossoms just coming into bloom.)
- 1 vanilla pod
- 1 piece of green tourmaline crystal

What gives you a sense of excitement or passion? What things make you feel as if you are lost in time, when nothing else matters to you except what you are doing? When is work no longer work, but becomes a joyful playtime?

If you have no idea, then wait to cast this spell until you know. Explore ideas, brainstorm with friends or partners, and seek out your true vocation.

Once you know, concentrate hard on your goal while you cast this spell.

Light the candle and place the blossoms alongside the vanilla pod and a piece of tourmaline on a table.

Hold the three blossom twigs in your hands as you say,

"I charge this blossom to invoke a new vocation or a successful career change into my life. So let it be."

Place the twigs back on the table and hold the vanilla pod, renowned for invoking a sense of peaceful power, for a few seconds in the candle flame. Say,

"I charge this candle to invite a new vocation or a successful career change into my life. So let it be."

Place the vanilla pod back on the table. Take the green tourmaline, a symbol of prosperity, and say,

"I charge this crystal to ignite success in all the changes I make. So let it be."

Let the candle burn all the way down before blowing it out. Leave your offerings overnight for the blossom spell to work its magic.

START SUCCESSFUL VENTURES

AN ENCHANTMENT TO MANIFEST SUCCESSFUL NEW VENTURES
When to Perform This Spell: The Night of Trivia (November 30)

The Roman goddess Trivia, equivalent to the Greek goddess Hecate, ruled over magic, sorcery, witchcraft, and divination. On the evening of the 30th, Romans left offerings to Trivia in the hope that she would transmit good news about their future via oracular priestesses in her temple who told futures by divining patterns found in candle wax. By invoking Trivia's power, you can successfully get started with any new ventures.

What You Will Need

3 rose hips (or rose hip tea)

3 nettle leaves (or nettle tea)

3 sprigs of rosemary

A bowl of ice-cold water

2 red candles

Raffia

Place the rose hips, nettle leaves, and sprigs of rosemary in the bowl of water. Bind together the two red candles (the color of desire) with the raffia (representing the manifest world). Stand the two candles in the bowl of water and light them. Now sit back and concentrate on the new business or wealth opportunity you are hoping for. If the wax doesn't drip easily, then hold the candles at an angle above the water.

Watch the patterns of wax forming in the water. When you are ready, say,

"Come hither, Trivia,
Come now to the crossroads of choice
Come, having one mind with me
Draw near, and bestow grace upon my desire."

Gaze at the wax patterns until one catches your eye and take it from the water. It may be attached to bigger patterns, so break the wax from the rest of the shapes and carefully place it on the table.

To manifest your desires, hold the wax shape in the palm of your hand and say the following spell:

"With Trivia's help good fortune comes.
With luck's desire and fire's truth
My flame of light has just begun."

Blow out the candles, relax, and within a few weeks you will begin to see new ventures and opportunities that will bring you success.

ATTRACT GOOD BUSINESS CONTACTS

AN ENCHANTMENT USING THE SYMBOL OF POPULUS
When to Perform This Spell: A Full Moon

By working with the power of the magical talisman Populus, you can attract both public attention and beneficial people to ensure good business.

Just after a new moon, draw or paint the symbol of Populus (see right) on a piece of paper and draw a circle around it to contain the energy flowing between the two parallel lines. If you want to make people stop and notice you, you must contain their energy in this corresponding way.

Fold the paper eight times (the number that activates corporate power and big business) and write on the last folded side, "with blessings to all." Leave this paper in a closed drawer.

Bury the eight small pieces of bloodstone in the ground, two inches deep if possible, in the same pattern as Populus. Burying crystals or gems taps into the natural magic of the earth, and bloodstones promote both courage and strength.

What You Will Need
A piece of paper and a pen or paint
8 small pieces of bloodstone
A covered box (optional)
Twine or cord

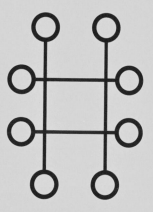

If you can't bury them, place them in the same pattern in a covered box placed somewhere it won't be disturbed. Whether buried or in a box, surround the two lines with a circle made of twine or cord.

After one week, remove one stone and carry it in your pocket or pouch until the next waxing moon; this will charge the stone with your personal charisma. At the full moon, return it to the remaining seven.

Keep safe both paper sigil and bloodstone symbols in their secret place for as long as you require. Soon you will be surrounded by people who can work their own personal magic for you, too.

MANIFEST SUCCESS

A SPELL CALLING ON MARS
When to Perform This Spell: The Spring Equinox (March 20)

This ancient Roman spell called on the powers of Mars and the element Fire, represented by the orange or gold candles, to create a potent mixture of positive energy to harness success.

What You Will Need
3 orange or gold candles
A small piece of paper and a pen

Place the candles in a triangle shape, which enhances their ability to work with the threefold power of Mars. Don't light the candles yet, but close your eyes and relax for a few moments and then say,

"Mighty Mars,
Thank you for all that I have.
I ask you now to help me manifest success.
Aid me as I work to achieve it.
Please bring it to me when the time is right.
So mote it be."

Draw the glyph for Mars, or Martis (see below), on the piece of paper three times, forming a triangle shape, and place the paper in the center of the three-candle triangle.

As you light each candle, say three times,

"Fire, ignite my dream for the highest good."

Concentrate on the triangle of candles for several minutes to draw on the energy and invoke the power of Mars.

Next, blow out the candles and thank Mars for his help on this equinox day.

"Thank you, Mars, for the power of success in my life."

Fold up the paper and go outside somewhere quiet and bury the paper in the ground or hide it beneath a large stone, boulder, or under a plant or tree. As you do so, say,

"Earth, seal my dream, for the highest good.
Air, follow my dream for the greatest good.
Water, nurture my dream for the highest good."

Within a few weeks, you should be in a position to manifest success.

SUCCEED IN BUSINESS

A SUCCESS POTION
When to Perform This Spell: Any time

In ancient Chinese traditions, Hsi Ho was the mythical mother of the sun. Every morning, she stretched out her son's golden arms to revitalize the Earth and bathed him in the east-shore lake so he would shine brightly throughout the day. This magic potion will draw business success, useful contacts, and deluxe living into your professional life. Use it as a room diffuser or spray it into the office to be like a magnet to the professional stars and shine as brightly as the sun itself.

A note about the ingredients: The Chinese mystics used many potions to attract wealth, wisdom, and power to the ancient dynastic families. It's not easy to find those ingredients, so this recipe is adapted to modern-day living. The ingredients may be a little expensive, but if you want to attract wealthy or luxury, you need to send that quality out to the universe.

What You Will Need

An 8-ounce (235 ml) glass jar or flacon with a lid

¼ cup (60 ml, or 2 ounces) pure spring water

¼ cup (60 ml, or 2 ounces) rosewater

Essential oils of:
Bergamot
Cinnamon
Lavender
Neroli
Rose
Geranium
Rosemary
Sandalwood
Cedar

Spray bottle

First, in the glass jar or flacon, mix equal parts of spring water and rosewater. Next add eight drops of each of the essential oils. Eight is an auspicious number in Chinese magic for business success. Don't worry if they don't mix in with the water, as the two invoke the power of the sun and the moon.

Put the top on the jar and shake vigorously. As you do, say,

"By the power of the Sun, let this potion prove
Some lavish success and wealth will move
By the power of the moon, good blessings will come
Draw business dreams to me, oh power of the One."

Use a funnel to empty some of the magic formula into a spray bottle, and then spray throughout your office, home, or business premises, concentrating particularly on thresholds, entrances, and doorways. You can even add it to your laundry rinse cycle (if you are not allergic to the ingredients) to permeate your clothes with its magical power of attracting luxury and success.

ENCOURAGE GREAT CONTACTS

A CHARM TO MAKE YOUR BUSINESS BETTER
When to Perform This Spell: A Full Moon

This charm is made up of a series of reinforcements, which will enable you to make your business even better. It will ensure that all those you meet are stunned by your talents and abilities.

To encourage a dynamic business life, place a piece of fire agate or ruby under your pillow or bed.

What You Will Need

1 piece of fire agate or ruby
1 large piece of fire agate
1 piece of aventurine
A piece of paper and a pen
1 piece of citrine

To attract good contacts to you, put as large a piece of agate as will fit on a window ledge where there is maximum moonlight to enhance your vitality.

For vitalizing ideas, creative thinking, and brainstorming success, place a piece of aventurine in your office desk or by your computer.

Once all your crystals are in place, do the following:

On the evening of the full moon, to maximize the culminating power of the lunar cycle, draw a row of three pentagrams (page 19) on a piece of paper, then place the paper with the tops of the pentagrams facing east. On top of the middle pentagram, lay the piece of citrine (the crystal of business and communication success) to attract abundance.

Every day for five days, take the citrine in your hands, focus hard for three minutes on what you really want most for a successful business, and place it back on the paper. Each time, repeat the following spell:

"By citrine bright
By citrine true
My business world will be ensured
Success and progress, both fulfilled."

After five days, purify the citrine by washing it in clear spring water and then leave it on a window ledge where it can attract the moon's powers for three nights. Now that it is charged with the moon's magic, carry it with you wherever you go in a small pouch or your bag. This will increase your business success threefold and will draw important new contacts to you, as well as potential deals or new goals.

THINK CREATIVELY

AN ENCHANTMENT TO AID CREATIVE THINKING
When to Perform This Spell: Modraniht (December 24)

The Modraniht, or "Mothers Night," was a pagan festival celebrating the triad of mother goddesses known as the Matres, whose energy will enable you to get in touch with your imagination and put on your creative "hat." It will also mean you can persuade anyone to your ideas, thoughts, or future plans, and it is also great if you are suffering from writer's block.

What You Will Need
3 white candles
A piece of paper and a pen
1 grèen leaf (or an image)
1 yellow flower (or an image)
1 blue flower (or an image)
A bowl of spring water

Place the candles in a triangle on your altar or table, light them, and sit quietly for a few moments to calm your mind.

Write down on the paper anything that bothers you, such as lack of creative thoughts, negative influences, and so on. Leave the paper beside the candles. Take up the green leaf and the yellow and blue flowers (or their images) in a bunch and hold them close to your "third eye" chakra—against the middle of your brow above your eyes—as you say the following:

"Blessed Matres, bring me magic charm
To move others without doing harm
Whereby the green, the yellow, and blue
Take not daggers, but speak only truth
So night and day, the stars and moon
Culminate in all that's done
And with this spell, so mote it be."

Place the flowers and leaf in the bowl of water and say,

"Thank you, Matres, for your help. Please send all creative thoughts my way."

Pass your hands, with your palms down, in a clockwise circle over the bowl and repeat the above thanks twice more as you do so. Within a few days, your creative flow will be empowered for the coming new year and your future plans.

GAIN NEW INSIGHTS

A SPELL TO EMPOWER YOU WITH CREATIVE WISDOM
When to Perform This Spell: Lughnasadh Sabbat (August 1)

Lughnasadh Sabbat, also known as Lammas, is the traditional Celtic celebration marking the beginning of the end of summer in the northern hemisphere, as well as the coming harvest. The Sabbat is about the cycle of birth, life, death, and rebirth when the Grain God dies, to be reborn in the spring. This day, call on the Great Goddess to nurture your own creativity or if you feel the need to finalize something in your life or "wrap up" unfinished business.

What You Will Need
1 small piece of obsidian
5 small pieces of peridot
1 red candle

Hold the piece of obsidian between both hands close to your chest and repeat the following blessing:

"With this stone I will grow in creative power
To become at one with the universe.
Thank you, Great Goddess, for blessing me with strength."

Now place the stone in an east corner of your home to promote and strengthen all affairs surrounding your own coming harvest of creativity.

On your altar or table, arrange five pieces of peridot (to enhance your powers or insight) in the pattern of the magic symbol Cauda Draconis, known as the dragon's tail, as shown at right. Five is the number of creativity, so for five evenings in a row, sit beside your altar, light the red candle, and gaze into the candle flame. One at a time, hold each piece of peridot close to your chest and repeat the following spell:

"God of Grain begone from sight.
It's time to harvest seeds of light.
Let Mother Earth bring ears of corn
That hear my thoughts and sound the horn.
Let Mother Earth bring fruitful pies
That I can eat to be so wise."

After one week, turn each stone 360 degrees clockwise once. After the second week, turn the stones 360 degrees counterclockwise. As you do, repeat the spell above and then add:

"Bless you, Mother Earth, Great Goddess, for the forthcoming creative harvest that I can now reap."

From now on, you can expect great thoughts, inspired meetings, new contacts, and abundant opportunities.

DEVELOP CREATIVE SKILLS

AN INVOCATION TO KAMALA
When to Perform This Spell: August 21

The Hindu goddess Lakshmi was known in one of her incarnations as Kamala, the goddess of wealth, creativity, and material beauty. She could be invoked to bring creative skills and was given offerings of rice and ghee. Drawing on her powers can bestow you with creative skill so that you too can fill your life with pleasure and wealth of every kind.

What You Will Need
5 white candles
A small bowl of rice

Light the five candles and place them in a circle on your altar or table to form the five points of a pentagram shape.

With the bowl of rice before you, place individual grains of rice on the altar in a circle about the size of a dinner plate. As you pick up a grain of rice and place it down, repeat the following spell until you have completed the circle:

"Kamala, bring me creative skill in work and play
For everlasting wealth in every day.
For art or craft, for thoughts or deeds
For success and health, and other needs
For pleasure, joy, and greater times
Let creativity be the guide to make life mine."

Once the spell is complete, take each grain of rice from the table and place it back in the bowl, one at a time. Repeat the spell again, and when you have finally replaced all the grains, thank the goddess by saying,

"Kamala, I give thanks to your divine power
To allow me to give grace to all creative enterprises, so mote it be."

Sit for a few minutes in relaxed silence by closing your eyes and thinking about your creative skill or the things you would like to be creative with. Then blow out the candles. To honor Kamala, scatter the rice in a river, stream, or lake.

NEGOTIATE SUCCESSFULLY

A SPELL TO FIND COMPROMISE AND HARMONY
When to Perform This Spell: A Full Moon

This full moon spell will help you with all forms of successful negotiations, particularly when you want to find compromise or be in harmony with others.

For this ritual, you will need a black piece of paper and a white crayon. Drawing the magic symbol Albus (see below) in white strengthens its power. Attach the white symbol to your mirror and every time you look at yourself, meditate for a few moments and imagine success pouring into a goblet. Beneficial influences and useful contacts will soon appear for your negotiation.

What You Will Need
A piece of black paper
A white pen or crayon
The magic symbol for Albus
7 small pieces or shards of white quartz crystal
Sage leaves, fresh or dried

Bury seven pieces of white quartz crystal in the ground in the symbol shape of Albus (or if you don't have access to a yard, place the pattern on the floor where it won't be disturbed). Sprinkle some sage leaves over the area for blessing and harmony and to protect it from negative energy. Walk around the pattern in a clockwise direction every day for seven days, repeating the mantra

"Harmony and negotiation will bring me justice and peace."

By the next full moon, you will be able to negotiate anything.

SELL YOUR IDEAS

AN ENCHANTMENT FOR CHARISMA
When to Perform This Spell: When the Sun Moves into Virgo (August 22)

As the sun moves into Virgo, we can cast spells that are progressive, shrewd, and insightful. With the help of runes—the powerful Norse symbols that are used as oracles and for invoking the power of the gods—you can sell yourself and your ideas, market your wares, or become so charismatic that you could sell ice to an Eskimo.

What You Will Need
7 smooth round pebbles or stones

Indelible pen or paint to mark the rune symbols on the stones

7 white tea light candles

A small box with a lid

On your table or altar, draw or paint the runic symbols found at the right onto the seven smooth pebbles.

The rune Ansuz will bring you wisdom. Hagalaz will activate the spell. Jera will help prove your value and worth. Dagaz brings positive transformation. Mannaz is for perfect communication. Wunjo is the rune of joy and ensures that the results of the spell will be a positive influence over others. Inguz allows the spell to last forever and prevents negative influence.

Light the candles, place them in a circle, and then take each stone in your hand one at a time and say,

"Bless you, gods of the runes, for my future success."

Place each stone beside a candle. When all are in place, walk around the table in a clockwise direction seven times (the number of runic magic). Finally, place the stones in a box and say the following to invoke the power of the gods:

"Ansuz, Laguz, gods of old
Let my powers of persuasion begin to unfold
That all that I say, write, or desire
Will bring me the dreams to which I aspire
That others will hear me, amazed and impressed
And my ideas will sell, for this I am blessed."

Let the tea lights extinguish on their own and then put the box in a safe place, preferably in a room or office where you work or do most of your business. (If you ever need to recharge your persuasive selling powers, take the stones out of the box and hold each of them for a few minutes while repeating the preceding spell.)

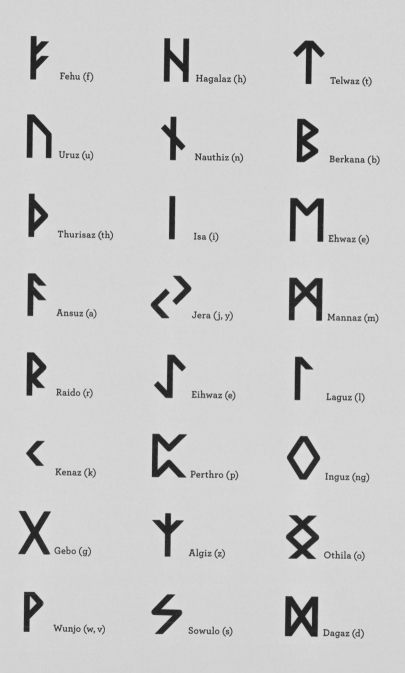

Fehu (f)

Hagalaz (h)

Telwaz (t)

Uruz (u)

Nauthiz (n)

Berkana (b)

Thurisaz (th)

Isa (i)

Ehwaz (e)

Ansuz (a)

Jera (j, y)

Mannaz (m)

Raido (r)

Eihwaz (e)

Laguz (l)

Kenaz (k)

Perthro (p)

Inguz (ng)

Gebo (g)

Algiz (z)

Othila (o)

Wunjo (w, v)

Sowulo (s)

Dagaz (d)

MONEY

How much would you like to earn?

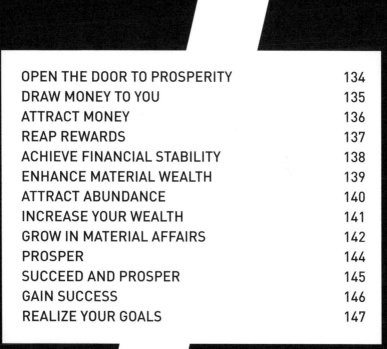

OPEN THE DOORWAY TO PROSPERITY

AN ENCHANTMENT CALLING ON JANUS AND DIANA
When to Perform This Spell: Janus and Diana's Festival (January 1)

Step into the new year with viable resolutions thanks to the goddess Diana and Janus, the Roman god of new beginnings. Diana was worshipped at countryside crossroads with gifts and offerings of fruit, while the power of Janus was invoked with salt and cakes placed on a sacred altar. For this spell, you'll combine those ingredients into one special enchantment.

Place the bag of earth in the center of your altar to invoke the power of Diana's abundance. Then place the three cupcakes in front of the bag and the tiny cup of salt in front of that. Now light the two candles to invoke your deities, and as you place them on either side of your offering, say or whisper the following:

What You Will Need

A handful of earth taken from each of the following places and gathered in a paper bag (if you can't get to any of these places, then three handfuls of earth from your own or a friend's garden will also work):

A crossroads

A forest, woods, or park

Beside a river, stream, or lake

3 cupcakes

A tiny cup of sea salt

2 white candles

"Diana, Janus, hear my prayer and bless this sacred altar.
For all year long let earth's riches empower me.
Let abundance bring me happiness.
Let your wholeness bring me prosperity."

Say this three times, and then thank your deities.

"Thank you, Diana, for your help.
Thank you, Janus, for your direction."

Now leave the candles burning for a few minutes while you gaze at your altar and calm your mind. Later, empty the bag of earth somewhere outside where you feel really happy to be, and as you sprinkle the earth on the ground, Janus and Diana will start to work the magic of prosperous living into your life.

DRAW MONEY TO YOU

A PROSPERITY SPELL
When to Perform This Spell: During the First Few Days After a New Moon

We would all like to have a little more cash flowing through our fingers. This medieval spell calls on the elemental spirits just after a new moon, when their powers will help you to attract to you what you truly need.

What You Will Need
1 white candle
Patchouli oil
1 silver-colored coin
4 pieces of malachite

During the first few days just after a new moon, rub a white candle with patchouli oil, then light it and place it on a table or your altar.

Gaze at the candle flame, relax, and think of money being drawn to you. Now put the coin in front of the candle, followed by the four malachite stones (for financial gain) around the candle and coin.

Now say,

"By the power of Air, Fire, Water, Earth
Let money come to me by good deeds done.
Let such be given generously, but harm come to none,
Multiply this coin, blessed spirits, for all my worth
So mote it be."

Sit quietly for a few more minutes while you gaze at the flame and try to imagine the money you truly need, rather than just want. Blow out the candle and carry the coin and the malachite stones with you in a pouch to maximize the rewards that are coming your way.

ATTRACT MONEY

AN ENCHANTMENT CALLING ON FORTUNA
When to Perform This Spell: At a Full Moon

This enchantment can help you when you really feel that you don't have enough money to get through the month. Remember not to use it for greed, but only for real need.

What You Will Need

7 strands of a fine natural thread, such as silk or cotton, about 1 foot (30 cm) to 2 feet (60 cm) long

Fortuna was the Roman goddess of luck, both good and bad, so if you want to ensure she brings you good luck, repeat to yourself that you need *"good luck"* in your life rather than just "luck."

Just before you go to bed, braid the seven strands of natural thread together. As you do so, repeat the following:

"Sweet goddess Fortuna, of fortune and luck,
Let money come to me this way
Without ill intent, for this I pray."

Repeat your spell over and over as you braid the strands. Repeat again as you tie nine knots all along the braided cord. Nine is the magic number of gold and also the number that brings truth and clarity.

As you tie the knots, visualize your financial needs being met. Keep repeating the spell out loud until you have tied the nine knots.

Place the knotted cord under your bed to encourage Fortuna's good luck in money into your life.

REAP REWARDS

A MONEY SPELL CALLING ON GANESHA
When to Perform This Spell: Any time

This enchantment for attracting money calls on the popular Hindu god of wise abundance, Ganesha. His magic powers will remove all obstacles in your pathway to making money, which will help to manifest your dreams.

On your table or altar, place the small mirror in the bottom of the bowl and add about 1 cup (235 ml) of water. Then place the candles in the water and light them. Next, surround your bowl with the red flowers. Take time to relax and then gaze into the mirror in the bowl.

What You Will Need

A small hand mirror

A clear glass bowl

Spring water

3 white floating candles

Red flowers such as camellias (Ganesha's symbol), carnations, or roses

Next, hold your hands with palms down over the bowl of candles (far enough away not to be burned or get hot!) and feel the energy from the reflected light. As you do this, repeat this spell three times:

"Oh, Ganesha, what was once lacking, it is time,
What was once wanting, will be mine,
What was once one, will become tenfold,
What was once tenfold, will be hundredfold,
What was once hundredfold, will become
Wealth and love to all around."

Relax, take a few slow deep breaths, and blow out the candles. Within a few weeks you will begin to reap the rewards of your efforts.

ACHIEVE FINANCIAL STABILITY

A CHARM FOR STABILITY AND YOUR POSITIVE PRESENCE
When to Perform This Spell: During a New Moon or Full Moon

As with many of the monthly new moon and full moon spells, this spell aligns with the astrological energy for the month in question but can also be performed at other new moons or full moons throughout the year.

Cover a small table with the silk or voile; blue is the color of the feng shui element Water, which symbolizes the West and prosperity. Hang up or lean a painting or photograph of waves at sea or a waterfall, so long as the water is "moving" (in order to keep money "flowing" in your direction).

What You Will Need

A piece of silk or voile in a shade of dark blue or aquamarine

A painting or photograph of moving water

2 pieces of blue agate or lapis lazuli

A small glass vessel

3 stems of three-leaf clover

1 piece of amber

Place the two pieces of blue agate or lapis lazuli in the small glass vessel to bring beneficial energy to all you do.

Place three stems of three-leaf clover (if you find any with four, that's even more auspicious) in the west corner of your home for three days and three nights to encourage financial stability.

Finally, carry a piece of amber to promote your positive presence in any environment.

ENHANCE MATERIAL WEALTH

A SPELL USING THE SIGIL CARCER
When to Perform This Spell: Any time

The magical number six and the geomantic sigil Carcer (see below) are both symbolic of strength, willpower, and stability. By drawing on the power of this magical combination, you can look forward to a more stable financial future.

What You Will Need
6 white quartz crystals
1 piece of black tourmaline
6 pieces of amethyst

Place six white quartz crystals, symbolizing confident decision making, in the shape of the Carcer symbol on a table, with a piece of black tourmaline in the middle (to enhance all material gain). For six days, move each of the quartz crystals one place forward to the next position in a counterclockwise direction. Then repeat the process for six days in a clockwise direction.

Each time you move a stone, say,

"Thank you Earth, and all the Stars
For this my state be True
That I can feel safe, endowed
With Wealth, in all I say and do."

This will activate the magic to make you feel empowered and ready to make your life more stable.

After twelve days of moving the crystals, place six pieces of amethyst (for progress) in a circle on your altar. Each day for six more days, place one of the white quartz stones alongside the amethysts, and finally place the black tourmaline in the center. This magic ritual will gradually bring you wealth and security and enhance financial, material, and family stability.

ATTRACT ABUNDANCE

AN ENCHANTMENT TO ATTRACT GOOD THINGS TO YOU
When to Perform This Spell: The Evening of a New Moon

This simple enchantment aligns you with the universe so that you can begin to attract good things into your life, whether new love, new job, new pleasure, or abundance.

What You Will Need
A white quartz crystal

Sit before your altar or table and hold the white quartz crystal between both your hands. Stay still for a while and concentrate on its vibrational universal energy charging you with light and love.

Now say the following spell:

"I am of earth, sun, moon, and stars.
I am of Jupiter, Venus, and Mars.
I am of spirits and phantom faces.
Of unknown worlds and far distant places.
I am of prophets, magi, and rainbows,
Of gold, copper, silver, and all that doth flow.
I am a child of the universe, divine, wild, and true.
And all goodness I give, will come back to me too."

Place the quartz crystal on the table and leave for one lunar cycle for the magic to work and bring you the things you seek.

INCREASE YOUR WEALTH

A SPELL FOR ENRICHMENT AND WEALTH
When to Perform This Spell: When the Sun Moves Into Cancer (June 22)

As the sun moves into Cancer, energy changes from solar to lunar, enhancing our sense of belonging and getting us in touch with how we can enrich our lives and achieve stability. Ruled by the moon, Cancer is also symbolic of security, wealth, and the spirit of enterprise. This charm draws on the power of the Celtic moon goddess, Arianrhod, whose name means "silver wheel." By invoking Arianrhod's powers, you will be ready to look to the future with fresh ideas to increase your wealth.

What You Will Need

A glass bowl, goblet, or chalice

Natural spring water

1 piece of green tourmaline, jade, malachite, or aventurine

Place the bowl, goblet, or chalice on a table, fill it nearly to the brim with natural spring water, and then sit quietly in front of it. Place your green crystal carefully at the bottom of the glass in the water. As you remove your hand from the water, with your index finger, draw a circle in a clockwise direction on the surface of the water as a magic circle of protection.

Close your eyes to calm your mind. When you are ready, open them and gaze into the water at the crystal, as if you are looking into your future. Then say,

"Arianrhod, please join me in this rite of prosperity. Please bring me your gifts, and for the good of everyone around me too."

Take the crystal out of the water and put it in a safe place in the southeast corner of your home. This is where beneficial solar energy aligns to the power of the crystal. Leave the crystal here for nine days to charge your home with feminine lunar power, nine being associated with the nine months of pregnancy.

After nine days, remove the crystal, put it in a pouch, and carry it with you to bring you beneficial wealth in all ways.

GROW IN MATERIAL AFFAIRS

A SPELL FOR POSITIVE GROWTH
When to Perform This Spell: New Year's Day for Trees (January 23)

Tu B'Shevat, the 15th of Shevat on the Jewish calendar, marks the beginning of a "new year" for trees. Casting this spell invokes the energy of a tree into your life: The oak tree is worshipped for its longevity; willows for the ability to adapt; rowan for success. Use this spell to invite trees' positive growth and symbolically conjure their beneficial cycles throughout the year.

What You Will Need
2 lengths of garden twine, 1 short, 1 long
A piece of paper and a pen

Remove three hairs from your head and tie them together with a short piece of twine. Take the bound hairs and a much longer piece of twine to an outdoor area that has trees. Walk around until you find a tree you like.

Tie your bound hair with the longer piece of twine. Then wrap the twine around the tree trunk as you say,

*"With hair and twine, my strength is yours, your strength is mine.
I am now bound to this sacred tree from toe to crown."*

Place your hands on the bark of the tree or literally "hug" the tree. Rest your head against the trunk for several minutes while you relax and draw on its strength and power. Then leave your hair and twine bound around the trunk.

When you get home, draw an image of the tree on a piece of paper. Write the five words below where the points of a pentagram would fall if you were to draw it over the tree.

Fold the paper up and place it in a safe place so that the power you have drawn from trees stays with you all year.

PROSPER

A FENG SHUI CHARM FOR PROSPERITY
When to Perform This Spell: Chinese New Year

Feng shui ("feng" meaning "wind" and "shui" meaning "water") is the Chinese art of placement for harmonious living. It is aligned to Taoist magic, dating back to 2000 BCE. In feng shui, the placement of crystals in your home corresponds to certain energies that will benefit your wealth and success. The northwest and west areas of your home correspond to success and prosperous living, while diamonds, selenite, white quartz, and silver all are symbolic of financial success.

First, create a sacred corner in the west or northwest corner of your home. This can be on a raised table, shelf, or window ledge. To make the area sacred, simply light a white candle and stand it in the corner. Now say,

What You Will Need

1 white candle

A silver gilt or silver-framed mirror

A silver chalice, cup, or bowl (pewter or stainless steel)

A silver or silver-colored necklace

1 diamond, piece of selenite, or white quartz crystal

A red envelope, packet, or sheet of red paper folded up, containing 3 silver or silver-colored coins

"Welcome to the deities of heaven and earth, and to the Jade Emperor, ruler of heaven."

To empower you with self-belief and added motivation for the rest of the year, place the silver-framed mirror against the wall and the silver vessel in front of the mirror. Drape a silver necklace around the mirror. Place a diamond, piece of selenite, or white quartz crystal in front of the mirror too, and in front of those, the red envelope (red is symbolic of success in Chinese tradition). These metal totems will improve your business and career dealings and bring you the success you deserve.

Remove all the items at the end of the following month and store safely away.

SUCCEED AND PROSPER

A SPELL CALLING ON OPS
When to Perform This Spell: Ops Festival (August 26)

This talismanic spell from the French Renaissance was allegedly used by a white witch who called on the power of Ops, the goddess of abundance, to help an idle scholar rise to fame as head librarian for the king of France and write a treatise on ancient coins. For your own privileged future, cast this spell between 6 p.m. and 9 p.m., when the goddess gave a silver coin to lost children and beggars.

What You Will Need

A small dish

A drawing of a pentacle

1 cinnamon stick

3 silver-colored coins

A wand (a stick, a twig, a baton, or anything wand-like)

A small pouch made of green velvet, linen, or silk

Place a small dish on the drawing of the pentacle on your altar or table and put in the cinnamon stick and the three coins. Just before you put each coin in the dish, tap it seven times with the wand as you say,

"Oh magical Ops, your silver coin of the moon,
Shine bright for us all, and bring me wealth soon.
Bring coins to my hands and tenfold grow strong,
Then tenfold again until tenfold be done."

Now with your wand, "stir" the air above the dish in a clockwise direction seven times and say,

"Fire, Earth, Water, Air, essence of light,
Antimony, vitriol, share treasure this night.
Share with me riches of silver and gold.
Success and prosperity, all will be shown."

Close your eyes for a few moments to let the beneficial energy come to you through the magic talisman. Put the coins and the cinnamon in the pouch and leave it somewhere safe overnight in the moonlight.

For the next lunar cycle (four weeks), either carry the bag with you or keep it near your bed where you will see it every night and know that it is working its magic for you.

GAIN SUCCESS

A SPELL TO DRAW MONEY TO YOU
When to Perform This Spell: Any time

Drawing on the power of the sun and moon, corresponding to gold and silver respectively, this is a simple spell to gain success in everything you intend to do in the next two weeks.

Place a red candle on one side of your room, and on the other side, place a white candle.

What You Will Need
| 1 red candle
| 1 white candle
| 1 gold-colored ring
| 1 silver-colored ring

First, light the red candle, then take the two rings in your right hand and pick up the red candle with your left hand. Walk in a straight line across the room directly to the white candle, and using the red one, light it. Set down the candles so they are side by side.

Now say,

"Sun with red and moon with white
Take this charm and make it right
So I may walk forth without doubt and fear,
As skies of success draw ever near."

Lay the two rings in front of the candles. (The gold ring in front of the white candle and the silver ring in front of the red candle will balance the magic ingredients.) Wait for the candles to burn halfway down and then take the two rings wherever you wish success to follow you.

For example, when you walk through the door for a job interview, remember how you walked in a straight line from the red candle to the white candle. Do the same as you make your way through the world to success.

REALIZE YOUR GOALS

A PROSPERITY SPELL CALLING ON BEFANA
When to Perform This Spell: The Festival of Befana (January 5)

Across Italy, the night before Epiphany is associated with the appearance of Befana, a witch who flies on a broomstick, enters houses through the chimney, and fills socks and shoes with sweets and presents. She sweeps the floor to clear away the problems of the year before departing. With this simple spell, you can ask Befana to make your home a prosperous one and to send you auspicious energy concerning your success and enterprises over the coming year.

What You Will Need

1 red candle placed on an altar or table

3 figs, 3 dates, or a small cup of honey

1 broom or brush

In the evening, place three figs or dates or a small cup of honey (traditional offerings to Befana) on a table beside the red candle.

Light the red candle, draw up a chair, and sit quietly for two minutes, gazing at the candle flame to still your mind and calm the energy around you. The red candle is a symbol of your own power to realize your goals, and it also calls upon the power of Befana. Now say the following out loud or in your head, three times:

"Come Befana, come to me
Come from the mountains to set me free
Come with your gifts of wisdom and cheer
To make this for me a most prosperous year."

Once you have repeated this spell three times, take the broom or brush and begin to sweep clockwise around the room toward a central spot to gather all Befana's beneficial energy in one place. Leave the broom and dust overnight.

Finally, blow out the candle, and as you do, thank Befana for her help:

"Thank you, Befana, for giving me the gifts of wisdom and prosperity."

The next day, remove the broom, clear up any dust or debris, and look forward to a hugely prosperous year.

PROTECTION

From what would you like to be safe?

ATTRACT BENEFICIAL LUCK

A SPELL CALLING ON ZEUS AND PANDIA
When to Perform This Spell: On the Eve of the Full Moon

In Greek mythology, Zeus was the god who decided your luck in life. If you made offerings to him, he usually bestowed you with good luck. Together with the moon goddess Selene, he had a beautiful daughter, Pandia, who was worshipped for her beneficial powers on the night of the full moon (believed to be the moment of her birth).

What You Will Need
1 red candle
1 piece of lapis lazuli
1 piece of turquoise
A ball of string
A pair of scissors
A silk scarf

Place and light the red candle, a symbol of potency, on the table, with the two stones on either side of the candle; the lapis lazuli is for hidden power and the turquoise is for exploiting ideas. Sit quietly before the table or altar on the eve of the full moon. Begin to unravel the string from the ball until it is as long as your arm. Then cut the string, place the length on the table, and say,

"By Pandia's power of moonlit night
Come bring me all that is my right.
And as this twine is cut each time
The luck of Zeus will be mine."

Repeat the string cutting nine more times (Zeus's number), saying the above spell each time.

When you have finished, say,

"Thank you, Zeus and Pandia, for helping me to have all that is due to me and for luck and stability in the future."

Leave the threads on the table overnight, but don't forget to blow out the candle! In the morning, take the threads and wrap them in a silk scarf. Keep them in a safe place so that you are blessed with good luck and long-term happiness.

BANISH BAD LUCK

A MIRROR ENCHANTMENT
When to Perform This Spell: On the Day of the Full Moon

In many traditions, ranging from Chinese feng shui to traditional European witchcraft, mirrors are used to ward off the evil eye or to banish negativity. This spell can take place anywhere—at work, out having fun, or staying at home—but you are going to banish negative energy around you so that good luck, harmony, and happiness come your way.

What You Will Need
Small vanity mirror

On the day of the full moon, take with you a small vanity mirror. Wherever you are, discreetly take the mirror in your hand and reflect all that is around you. This removes negativity and causes no harm to anyone.

When you get home, place the mirror face down in a place where no one else can pick it up, or wrap it in black fabric and put it in a drawer overnight.

As you do so, say,

"Planets, Earth, Air, Water, Fire
Aligned to bring my heart's desire:
Bad luck turn and bad luck flee.
Good luck and fortune comes to me."

The next morning in daylight, take the mirror outside, hold it up to face the direction of the sun for nine seconds (the number of universal reward), and the negativity will be burned away and replaced by positive solar energy to bring you good luck.

BANISH FEAR

A SPELL FOR SWAPPING FEAR FOR OPPORTUNITIES
When to Perform This Spell: Just After the Full Moon

This spell will help you overcome any fears you have, swapping fear for opportunities to be seized. The sacred book you use can be any book you value—a Bible, a much-loved sacred text, or a novel that has "changed" you in some way.

What You Will Need

A sacred book

Frankincense incense

An iron or metal bell

A piece of paper and a pen

Place the book on your table or altar and randomly open it to a page. Don't look at the page yet. Light the incense to banish all forms of stress, worry, and difficult emotions.

Now ring the bell three times to cast out unwanted fears. Place it back on the table and sit before your book. Close your eyes and with one finger, begin to make circles in the air over the open book. When you feel compelled to stop, place your finger randomly on the page. Open your eyes and look to where your finger is pointing.

Take the whole sentence, or even two sentences together, and write them down on a piece of paper. These words are an oracle and will banish all fear from you forever if you keep the paper in a safe place. If ever you feel fearful, read the words again or perform the spell again.

BANISH BAD ENERGY

A SPELL FOR GETTING RID OF UNWANTED ENERGY
When to Perform This Spell: Just After the Full Moon

Use this spell to get rid of any unwanted energy in your life. This ancient magic square was once used to ward off all manner of evil. It will enable you to get rid of all that is unwanted in your life and help bring you all that you want to manifest.

What You Will Need
A piece of paper
A pen
5 red candles

On the paper, write down this magic word square:

S A T O R
A R E P O
T E N E T
O P E R A
R O T A S

Place a candle on the first letter of each line of the square from top to bottom and say the magic words,

"Sator, Arepo, Tenet, Opera, Rotas,
By the power of words all bad be gone.
By the power of words all wrongs be gone.
By the power of words all negativity be gone.
So mote it be."

Move the candles now to the last letter at the end of each line and finally light them. Now say the magic charm again. and sit for a few moments gazing into the candle flames before you blow them out. All negativity will be gone.

BANISH NEGATIVITY

A SPELL TO BANISH EVIL AND ENCOURAGE POSITIVE ENERGY
When to Perform This Spell: Chinese Dragon Boat Festival
(Any point between the 1st and 15th of June)

The Dragon Boat Festival commemorates the attempt to rescue Qu Yuan, a third–century BCE Chinese scholar falsely accused of conspiracy who drowned himself in the Miluo River during his exile. Traditionally, the festival included charms and talismans, including perfumed sachets, to banish evil in one's life and encourage positive energy. "Noon water," or water collected at noon, was a way to purify and cleanse the home. Today, people hang pictures of the deity Zhong Kui, vanquisher of ghosts and evil spirits, on the door of their homes. This general spell banishes all negativity from your life by drawing on the power of Zhong Kui.

What You Will Need

1 black candle

Sandalwood incense

A wand, wooden stick, or athame

A chalice or goblet filled with water

A piece of paper

A black pen

Place the black candle and other tools on a table or on the ground so everything is ready.

Before invoking the power of Zhong Kui, cast a circle around yourself and the magic tools and call in the spirits of the four quarters for protection as described on page 19. Within your magic circle, light the candle and the incense and invite Zhong Kui to join you by saying,

"Zhong Kui, guardian of all, protector from negativity, please join me as I seek to banish all negative energy from my life."

Take up your wand or athame and point it at the chalice or goblet of water. Close your eyes and imagine a pure white light coming down from the sky, as you draw on the spirit powers. Repeat the following:

"By all Zhou's power and wondrous light
Be gone all evil from my life
All negative thoughts are sent away
That positive ones will only stay."

Now sit down and write on the paper with your pen all the things you want to banish from your life. They may be emotions such as anger and jealousy or people whom you no longer want to know. They may be feelings of loss or problems with money or debt. Whatever it is that is negative about your life, write it down. Fold the paper up four times and place it beside the chalice. Now say,

"All negativity be gone
All wrongs be gone
All bad things be gone
All that is dark be turned to light
All that is night be turned to day
All that is bright come to my life."

Next, pick up the chalice and drink some of the water, but not all of it. Place the paper into the rest of the sacred water, where you will leave it until noon the next day. Release Zhou from the spell by saying,

"Thank you, Zhou, hunter of negativity, vanquisher of all that is dark or bad, thank you for helping me to move on."

Release the spirits by bowing to each of the four directions and giving thanks, then blow out the candle.

The next day, go back to where you left the chalice of water. Exactly at noon, take the paper out of the water, tear it up into shreds, and throw it away, then throw away the water. As you throw it away, you are ridding your life of everything bad.

PROTECT AGAINST NEGATIVITY

A CHARM FOR SUCCESSFUL PERSONAL AFFAIRS
When to Perform This Spell: Lucaria Roman Feast (July 19)

The Romans celebrated the Lucaria as the last part of an ancient rite, which had begun back in May to banish all evil spirits from the home. The celebration occurred in a sacred grove and called on all spirits of the woods, forests, and lands for protection in the home and for the coming harvest. This spell will protect your home from negativity and give you the energy and self-confidence to attend to your work or career free from family worries.

What You Will Need

2 pieces of paper and a pen

1 silver-colored ring

1 piece of tiger's-eye

A few marigolds or dried marigold leaves

On the first piece of paper, write the following and fill in the blanks.

I am really PLEASED when I

I ADORE

I'm FASCINATED by

I ENJOY

I am GRATEFUL for

I WANT

WARM feelings come to me when

I FEEL JOY when

I INTEND to

My PURPOSE is

Fold this up and place it aside.

Now take the other piece of paper and draw an imaginary sacred grove. It can be just a circle with symbols to represent trees or spirits, or it can be more elaborate. But whatever comes into your imagination is important, because the power of magic works through our ability to imagine things, and then to believe they will happen.

Now place the silver ring and the tiger's-eye in the center of the "sacred grove" to represent the power of self-confidence and family happiness.

As you do so, say,

"To the spirits of the sacred grove, let my home and family be blessed with your protection while I carry out all that I must do for myself."

Finally, sprinkle some of the marigolds (renowned for their regenerative and protective properties) in all four corners of your home—north, south, east, and west. With the ritual complete, you can now look forward to getting on with your personal mission, and your family or home will be safe from outside influence.

END GOSSIP

A RITUAL CALLING ON THE SUN
When to Perform This Spell: As the Sun Moves into Leo (July 22)

Leo is about pride, about being sure of yourself, and about not letting others hurt you. This spell is based on the execution of the Duke of Clarence for treason against his brother, King Edward IV. The duke was supposedly drowned, at his request, in a barrel of Malmsey wine! Here you'll "drown" negativity or antisocial behavior, as well as rid yourself of those who are two-faced, backbiters, or gossipmongers.

Place the items on your table or altar and light the white candle. With the pen, write on the slip of paper the nature of the antisocial behavior, but not the person's name.

Fold the paper in half and as you do so, say,

"With this spell I stop your malice.
With this spell I keep my wholeness.
Your reign of power is over and done.
I work this spell with harm to none."

What You Will Need

1 white candle

A slip of paper

A black pen

A jam jar and lid

1 tablespoon (9 g) garlic powder

1 tablespoon (6 g) black pepper

1 glass of wine

Drop the paper into the jar and add the garlic powder and black pepper to banish negativity. Then pour in the wine to cover the paper. Screw the lid in place and keep the jar by your altar or inside your front door, where every time you pass, the magic will be increased threefold. You should start seeing positive results within a couple of weeks.

PROTECT YOUR GOALS FROM INTERFERENCE

A SPELL TO KEEP RIVALS FROM BLOCKING YOU
When to Perform This Spell: Any time

This spell first stops rivals from blocking or preventing you from your goal and means that any form of achievement can be all yours. This spell calls on the spirits of nature and spring to sprinkle you with their blessings to achieve your best.

On the piece of paper, write down the names of those people you want to block, then cross out their names and write your own in much larger writing across all their names. As you do so, say,

"I cross you, I banish you
I cover you, I command you
All who do not deserve to have luck with me
Be gone now, so mote it be."

What You Will Need

A piece of paper and a pen
1 purple candle
Lavender oil
A small dish
1 basil plant or sprigs of basil
A paper bag

Take the purple candle and rub a little lavender oil down the sides of the candle to bless it. Place the paper of names on a dish and the candle on top of the paper, then light the candle.

While the candle is burning, take the basil sprigs in your hands and pick as many leaves as there are names on your banishment list. Basil is protective, restorative, generative, and empowering, and it keeps away unwanted spirits, people, and energies.

As you do so, say,

"As nature stirs again
I ask the spirits of spring to bless me with personal achievement and success
See that it comes to me, and me alone."

Blow out the candle, place the basil leaves in a paper bag, and throw the bag into the trash. This symbolic action means you will now achieve all you set out to do alone, without the interference of anyone you have written on your list.

PROTECT YOUR TRAVELS

A SPELL TO BRING BENEFICIAL INFLUENCES ON YOUR JOURNEY
When to Perform This Spell: Winter Solstice (December 21)

What You Will Need

2 pieces of aquamarine
3 pieces of beryl
A small pouch
A small kitchen knife
1 white candle
Frankincense incense

We all want to leave home at some point in our lives. By invoking the protective powers of Ops, the earth goddess married to Saturn, you can make your time away positive. When Romans traveled, they often carried a small sheaf of corn (Ops's main attribute) for protection or placed it on the threshold of their home to ensure a safe return.

First, sit quietly, relax, and concentrate on your destination. Take the pieces of aquamarine and beryl (both protective talismans when traveling) and place them in the pouch.

With the knife, carve into the side of the candle the name of the place you are going to visit.

Light the candle and the incense and pass the pouch back and forth seven times through the smoke of the incense to invoke the help of Ops. Concentrate on the candle flame. Now open the pouch, take out the five stones, and place them in a circle around the candle.

Say the following,

"Wherever I go in the East,
This heart of my home will never be least.
Wherever I go in the North,
There will always be time to again set forth.
Wherever I go in the South,
This heart of my home will be a safe path.
Wherever I go in the West,
From now on my travels will be for the best."

Thank Ops for her help and then take the five stones and place them back in the pouch. Carry them with you on your travels for protection and safe homecoming.

APPENDIX

Many of the spells in this book work best at the right moment during the wheel of the year. Others work any time, or during particular parts of the lunar cycle. Use this calendar to plan your date-specific spellwork.

FULL MOON

NEW MOON

ANY TIME

EPILOGUE

My Sorceress lives with the sun and the stars,

She sleeps by the falls of Venus and Mars

And her heart is drawn by the sway of the Moon

When whispers of love can beckon too soon.

Stern Saturn guides her to know her place

When the Winds of Chaos line energy's face,

And Jupiter holds her and kisses her now

As she trickles clear water on Neptune's brow.

For her head is turned by Mercurial charm,

And the eyes to her soul are peculiarly armed

With Uranian light that has seen Pluto's hell,

For who is she, but just a child of my spell?

ACKNOWLEDGMENTS

Thanks to everyone at Fair Winds Press for making this book so beautiful; especially Jill Alexander for her personal magic, and Jennifer Kushnier for her bewitching advice. I also want to thank my agent, Chelsey Fox, for her eternal support, and my family for being who they are and believing in the magic of the universe.

ABOUT THE AUTHOR

Sarah Bartlett is the author of more than twenty psycho-spiritual non-fiction books, including the best-selling Tarot Bible. She has been astrologer for the London Evening Standard, Cosmopolitan, She, and Spirit and Destiny. She is also one of the founder members of www.theastrologyroom.com, where she provides both weekly content and a consultation service.

After studying for an art degree at Middlesex University in London, Sarah went on to become a consultant astrologer, first training at the Faculty of Astrological Studies in London, and then acquiring the diploma in psychological astrology at the Centre for Psychological Astrology, an in-depth, three-year professional training program that cross-fertilizes the fields of astrology, mythology and depth, and humanistic and transpersonal psychology.

Sarah currently contributes as astrologer to the Steve Wright in the Afternoon Show on BBC Radio 2 and divides her time between London and the South of France, where she teaches and practices the occult arts.

INDEX